Aunt Phil's Trunk Volume Four

Teacher Guide

Bringing Alaska's history alive!

By
Laurel Downing Bill

Special credit and much appreciation to Nicole Cruz for her diligent efforts to create the best student workbook and teacher guide available for Alaska history studies.

Aunt Phil's Trunk LLC, Anchorage, Alaska
www.auntphilstrunk.com

Copyright © 2017 by Laurel Downing Bill.

All rights reserved. No part of this book may be used or reproduced in any manner whatsoever without written permission from the author, except in the case of brief quotations embodied in critical articles and reviews.

International Standard Book Number 978-1-940479-30-9
Printed and bound in the United States of America.

First Printing 2017
First Printing Second Edition 2017
First Printing Third Edition 2018

Photo credits on the front cover, from top left: Native shaman with totem, Alaska State Library, Case and Draper Collection, ASL-P-39-782; Eskimo boy, Alaska State Library, Skinner Foundation, ASL-P44-11-002; Prospector, Alaska State Library, Skinner Foundation, ASL-P44-03-15; Athabascan woman, Anchorage Museum of History and Art, Crary-Henderson Collection, AMHA-b62-1-571; Gold miners, Alaska State Library, Harry T.Becker Collection, ASL-P67-052; Chilkoot Pass, Alaska State Library, Eric A. Hegg Collection, ASL-P124-04; Seal hunter, Alaska State Library, George A. Parks Collection, ASL-P240-210; Women mending boat, Alaska State Library, Rev. Samuel Spriggs Collection, ASL-P320-60; Teacher photo, Alaska State Library, J. Simpson MacKinnon Photo Collection, ASL-P14-073.

TABLE OF CONTENTS

Instructions *Aunt Phil's Trunk* Alaska History Curriculum	5
How to use this workbook at home	6
How to use this workbook for high school	7
How to use this workbook in the classroom	8
How to grade assignments	9
Rubric for Essay Questions	11
Rubric for Oral Presentations	12
Rubric for Enrichment Activities	12

UNIT 1: WORLD WAR II ERUPTS

Lesson 1: Defense for Alaska	13
Lesson 2: Russia's Secret Mission	15
Lesson 3: Army Base Revitalizes Anchorage	17
Review Lessons 1-3	19
Unit Test	22

UNIT 2: MILITARY ROUTES EMERGE

Lesson 4: Railroader Tunnels to Whittier	24
Lesson 5: Road Heads North to Alaska	26
Lesson 6: Outposts Spout Up	26

UNIT 3: A FEW GOOD MEN

Lesson 7: Eskimo Scouts Volunteer	30
Lesson 8: The Flying Baritone from Fairbanks	33
Lesson 9: J. Doolittle: Nome Town Boy	35
Review Lessons 4-9	38
Unit Test	44

UNIT 4: CONFLICT IN THE ALEUTIANS

Lesson 10: Dutch Harbor Attacked	47
Lesson 11: Enemy Invades Attu	49
Lesson 12: Japanese Americans Interred	52
Lesson 13: Aleuts Become Refugees	54
Lesson 14: Enemy Ousted From Aleutians	56
Review Lessons 10-14	58
Unit Test	62

TABLE OF CONTENTS

UNIT 5: 1940s POSTWAR NEWS
   Lesson 15: 1945: Discrimination Torpedoed   65
   Lesson 16: 1947: Reeve Airways Takes Flight   67
   Lesson 17: 1948: Murderer Nominated King   69
   Lesson 18: 1948: Alaska Airlines Makes History   71
   Lesson 19: In Other News ...   73
   Review Lessons 15-19   74
   Unit Test   78

UNIT 6: COLD WAR ERA
   Lesson 20: 'Red Scare' Brings Boom   80
   Lesson 21: Anchorage: Jewel on the Tundra   82
   Lesson 22: Other Alaska Towns Grow   84
   Lesson 23: Tuberculosis: The Alaska Scourge   86
   Review Lessons 20-23   90
   Unit Test   92

UNIT 7: ROAD TO STATEHOOD
   Lesson 24: Movers & Shakers   94
   Lesson 25: Statehood Momentum Builds   96
   Lesson 26: Egan: The Final Push   98
   Review Lessons 24-26   100
   Unit Test   104

UNIT 8: STATEHOOD AT LAST
   Lesson 27: Black Gold Tips the Balance   106
   Lesson 28: We're In!   108
   Lesson 29: 'Simple Flag of the Last Frontier'   110
   Review Lessons 27-29   114
   Unit Test   116

Teacher notes   118-120

Welcome to *Aunt Phil's Trunk Volume Four* Teacher Guide!

Read the chapters associated with each Unit. Then complete the lessons for that Unit to get a better understanding of Alaska's people and the events that helped shape Alaska's future.

I hope you enjoy your journey into Alaska's past from the years 1935 to 1960.

Laurel Downing Bill, author

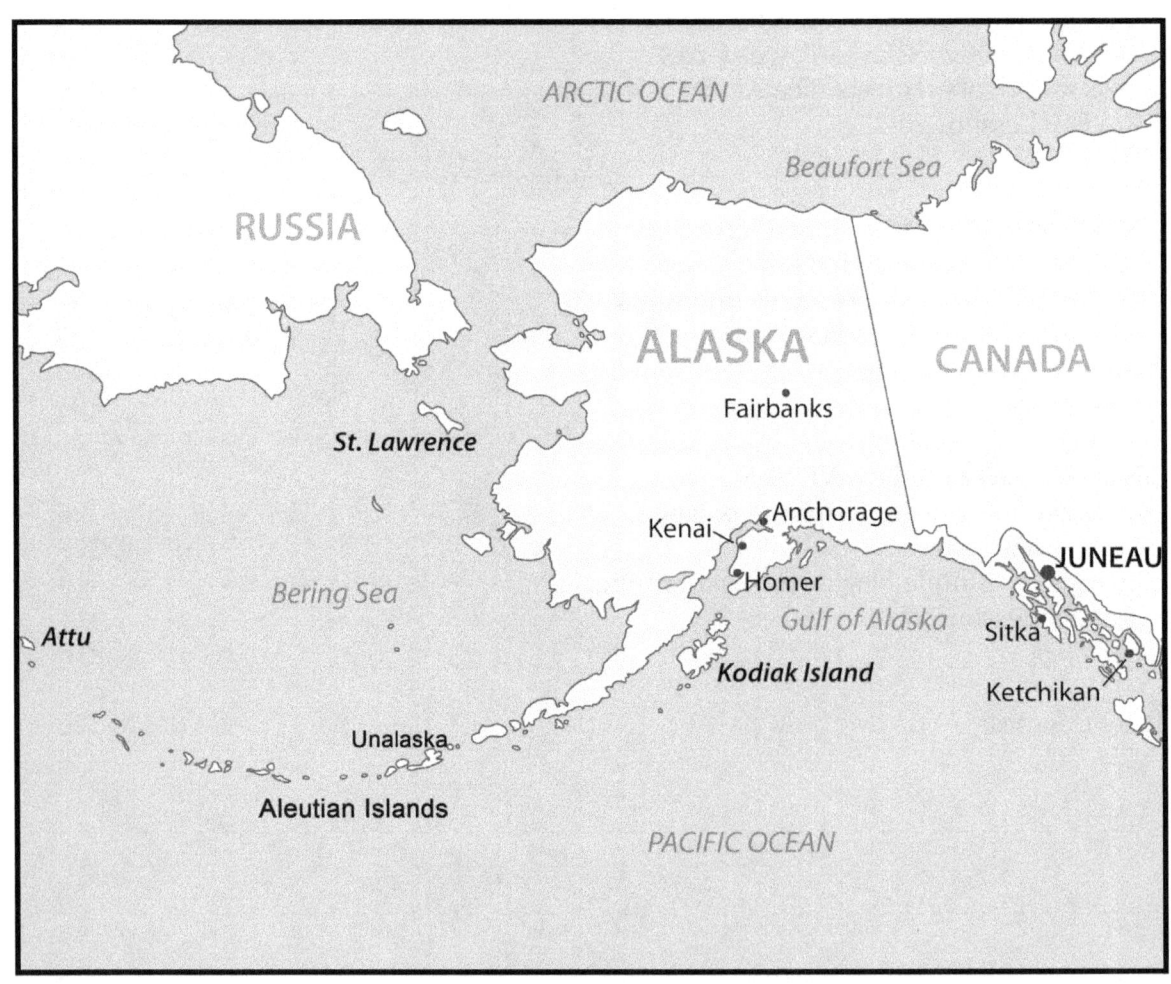

Instructions for using the Aunt Phil's Trunk Alaska History Curriculum

The *Aunt Phil's Trunk* Alaska History Curriculum is designed to be used in grades 4-8. High school students can use this curriculum, also, by taking advantage of the essay and enrichment activities throughout the book. The next few pages give further instruction on how to use this curriculum with middle school students, high school students and in classroom settings.

This curriculum can be taught in multiple grade levels by having your older students complete all reading, study guide work and enrichment activities independently. Students of all grade levels can participate in daily oral review by playing games like Jeopardy or Around the World.

This curriculum was developed so that students not only learn about Alaska's past, but they will have fun in the process. After every few lessons, they can test their knowledge through word scramble, word search and crossword puzzles.

Notes for parents with younger students:

Enrichment Activities occasionally direct your child to watch educational videos on YouTube.com or link to other Websites to learn more about the topic that they are reading about in the lesson. You may want to supervise younger children while they are using the Internet to be sure that they do not click on any inappropriate content. This also provides a good opportunity to discuss Internet safety with your child/children.

How to use this workbook at home

Aunt Phil's Trunk Alaska History Curriculum is designed to be used in grades 4-8. High school students can use this curriculum, also, by taking advantage of the essay and enrichment activities throughout the book. The next page gives further instruction on how to use this curriculum with high school students.

This curriculum can be taught in multiple grade levels by having your older students complete all reading, study guide work and enrichment activities independently. Students of all grade levels can participate in daily oral review by playing games like Jeopardy or Around the World.

For Middle School Students:

1. **Facts to Know:** Read this section in the study guide with your student(s) before reading the chapter to get familiar with new terms that they will encounter in the reading.

2. **Read the chapter:** Read one chapter aloud to your student(s) or have them read it aloud to you. Older students may want to read independently.

3. **Comprehension Questions:** Younger students may answer the comprehension questions orally or write down their answers in the study guide. Use these questions to test your student(s) comprehension of the chapter. Older students should answer all questions in written form.

4. **Discussion Questions:** Have your student(s) answer these questions in a few sentences orally. Come up with follow-up questions to test your student(s) understanding of the material. Older students may answer discussion questions in written essay form.

5. **Map Work:** Some chapters will contain a map activity for your student(s) to learn more about the geography of the region that they are learning about.

6. **Enrichment and Online References:** (Optional) Assign enrichment activities as you see fit. Many of the online references are from the Alaska Humanities Forum website (http://www.akhistorycourse.org). We highly recommend this website for additional information, project ideas, etc.

7. **Unit Review:** At the end of a unit, your student will complete Unit Review questions and word puzzles in the study guide. Students should review all the chapters in the unit before completing the review. Parents may want to assist younger students with the word puzzles.

8. **Unit Test:** (Optional) There is an optional test that you can administer to your student(s) after they have completed all the unit work.

How to use this workbook for high school

1. **Facts to Know:** Your student(s) should read this section in the study guide before reading the chapter to get familiar with new terms that they will encounter.

2. **Read the chapter:** Your student(s) can read aloud or independently.

3. **Comprehension Questions:** Use these questions to test your student(s) comprehension of the chapter. Have your high schoolers write out their answers in complete sentences.

4. **Discussion Questions:** Have your student(s) answer these questions in a few sentences orally or write out their answer in essay form.

5. **Map Work:** Some chapters will contain a map activity for your student(s) to learn more about the geography of the region that they are learning about.

6. **Enrichment and Online References:** Once your high schooler has completed all the reading and study guide material for the chapter, assign additional reading from the enrichment material using the online links or book lists. Encourage your student(s) to explore topics of interest to them.

Many of the online references are from the Alaska Humanities Forum website. We highly recommend this website for additional information, project ideas, etc.

7. **Unit Review:** At the end of a unit, your student will complete Unit Review questions and word puzzles in their study guide. Students should review all the chapters in the unit before completing the review.

8. **Unit Test:** (Optional) There is an optional test that you can administer to your student(s) after they have completed all the unit work.

9. **Oral Presentation:** (Optional) Assign a 5-minute oral presentation on any topic in the reading. Encourage your student(s) to utilize the additional books and online resources to supplement the information in the textbook. Set aside a classroom day for your student(s) to share their presentations.

10. **Historical Inquiry Project:** Your student(s) will choose a topic from the reading to learn more about and explore that topic through library visits, museum trips, visiting historical sites, etc.

Visit https://www.nhd.org/how-enter-contest for detailed information on how to put together a historical inquiry project. You may even want to have your students enter the national contest.

How to use this workbook in the classroom

Aunt Phil's Trunk Alaska History Curriculum was created for homeschooling families, but it also can work well in a co-op or classroom setting. Here are some suggestions on how to use this curriculum in a classroom setting. Use what works best for your classroom.

1. **Facts to Know:** The teacher introduces students to the Facts to Know to familiarize the students with terms that they will encounter in the chapter.

2. **Read the chapter:** The teacher can read the chapter aloud while the students follow along in the book. Students also may take turns reading aloud.

3. **Comprehension Questions:** The teacher uses these questions to test the students' comprehension of the chapter. Students should write out the answers in their study guide and the teacher can review the answers with the students in class.

4. **Discussion Questions:** The teacher chooses a few students to answer these questions orally during class. Alternatively, teachers can assign these questions to be completed in essay form individually and answers can be shared during class.

5. **Map Work:** Some chapters will contain a map activity for your students to learn more about the geography of the region that they are learning about. Have your students complete the activity independently.

6. **Enrichment and Online References:** Assign enrichment activities as you see fit.

7. **Daily Review:** Students should review the material for the current unit daily. You can do this by asking review questions orally. Playing review games like Jeopardy or Around the World is a fun way to get your students excited about the material.

8. **Unit Review:** At the end of a unit, your student will complete Unit Review questions and word puzzles in the study guide. Have students review all the unit chapters before completing.

9. **Unit Test:** (Optional) There is an optional test that you can administer to your students after they have completed all the unit work.

10. **Oral Presentation:** (Optional) Assign a 5-minute oral presentation on any topic in the reading. Encourage your students to utilize the additional books and online resources to supplement the information in the textbook. Set aside a classroom day for students to share their presentations.

11. **Historical Inquiry Project:** Your student(s) will choose a topic from the reading to learn more about and explore that topic through library visits, museum trips, visiting historical sites, etc.

Visit https://www.nhd.org/how-enter-contest for detailed information on how to put together a historical inquiry project. You may even want to have your students enter the national contest.

How to grade the assignments

Our rubric grids are designed to make it easy for you to grade your students' essays, oral presentations and enrichment activities. Encourage your students to look at the rubric grid before completing an assignment as a reminder of what an exemplary assignment should include.

You can mark grades for review questions, essay tests and extra credit assignments on the last page of each unit in the student workbook. Use these pages as a tool to help your students track their progress and improve their assignment grades.

Unit Review Questions

Students are given one point for each correct review and fill-in-the-blank question. Mark these points on the last page of each unit in the student workbook.

Essay Test Questions

Students will complete two or more essay questions at the end of each unit. These questions are designed to test your students' knowledge about the key topics of each unit. You can give a student up to 20 points for each essay.

Students are graded on a scale of 1-5 in four categories:

1) Understanding the topic
2) Answering all questions completely and accurately
3) Neatness and organization
4) Grammar, spelling and punctuation

Use the essay rubric grid on page 11 as a guide to give up to 5 points in each category for every essay. Mark these points for each essay on the last page of each Unit Review in the student workbook.

Word Puzzles

Word puzzles that appear at the end of the Unit Reviews count for 3 points, or you can give partial points if the student does not fill in the puzzle completely. Mark these points under the extra category on the last page of each Unit Review in the student workbook.

Enrichment Activities

Most lessons contain an enrichment activity for further research and interaction with the information in the lesson. You can make these optional or assign every activity as part of the lesson. You can use the provided rubric on page 12 to give up to 5 points for each assignment. Mark these points under the extra category on the last page of each Unit Review in the student workbook.

Oral Presentations

You have the option of assigning oral presentations on any topic from the unit as extra credit. If you choose to assign oral presentations, you can use the provided rubric to grade your student on content and presentation skills. Discuss what presentation skills you will be grading your student on before each presentation day.

Some examples of presentation skills you can grade on include:

- Eye contact with the audience
- Proper speaking volume
- Using correct posture
- Speaking clearly

Use the oral presentation rubric grid on page 12 as a guide to give up to 10 points. Mark these points under the extra category on the last page of each Unit Review in the student workbook.

Rubric for Essay Questions

	Beginning 1	Needs Improvement 2	Acceptable 3	Accomplished 4	Exemplary 5
Demonstrates Understanding of the topic	Student's work shows incomplete understanding of the topic	Student's work shows slight understanding of the topic	Student's work shows a basic understanding of the topic	Student's work shows complete understanding of the topic	Student's work demonstrates strong insight about the topic
Answered questions completely and accurately	Student's work did not address all of the questions	Student answered all of the questions with some accuracy	Student answered all questions with close to 100% accuracy	Student answered all questions with 100% accuracy	Student goes beyond the questions to demonstrate knowledge of the topic
Essay is neat and well organized	Student's work is sloppy and unorganized	Student's work is somewhat neat and organized	Student's essay is neat and somewhat organized	Student's work is well organized and neat	Student demonstrates extra care in organizing the essay and making it neat
Essay contains good grammar and spelling	Student's work is poorly written and hard to understand	Student's work contains some grammar, spelling and punctuation mistakes, but not enough to impede understanding	Student's work contains only 1 or 2 grammar, spelling or punctuation errors	Student's work contains no grammar, spelling or punctuation errors	Student's work is extremely well-written

Rubric for Oral Presentations

	Beginning 1	Needs Improvement 2	Acceptable 3	Accomplished 4	Exemplary 5
Preparation	Student did not prepare for the presentation	Student was somewhat prepared for the presentation	Student was prepared for the presentation and addressed the topic	Student was well-prepared for the presentation and addressed important points about the topic	Student prepared an excellent presentation that exhibited creativity and originality
Presentation Skills	Student demonstrated poor presentation skills (no eye contact, low volume, appears disinterested in the topic)	Student made some effort to demonstrate presentation skills (eye contact, spoke clearly, engaged audience, etc.)	Student demonstrated acceptable presentation skills (eye contact, spoke clearly, engaged audience, etc.)	Student demonstrated good presentation skills (eye contact, spoke clearly, engaged audience, etc.)	Student demonstrated strong presentation skills (eye contact, spoke clearly, engaged audience, etc.)

Rubric for Enrichment Activities

	Beginning 1	Needs Improvement 2	Acceptable 3	Accomplished 4	Exemplary 5
	Student's work is incomplete or inaccurate	Student's work is complete and somewhat inaccurate	Student completed the assignment with accuracy	Student's work is accurate, complete, neat and well-organized	Student demonstrates exceptional creativity or originality

UNIT 1: WORLD WAR II ERUPTS

LESSON 1: DEFENSE FOR ALASKA

FACTS TO KNOW

Pearl Harbor – Hawaiian port that was attacked with bombs by Japan on December 7, 1941

President Franklin D. Roosevelt – The 32nd president of the United States who declared war on Japan after the bombing of Pearl Harbor

COMPREHENSION QUESTIONS

1) How many Americans were killed during the attack on Pearl Harbor? What other damage was done? _Within two hours, the sneak attack had killed 2,402 Americans, destroyed five battleships, put three out of commission, sank or damaged almost a dozen other warships and obliterated more than 180 aircraft on the ground. In addition to Pearl Harbor, Japan also attacked the U.S. territory of Guam, the Philippines, Wake Island and Midway Island the next day, as well as British interests in Malaya and Hong Kong._ (Page 9)

2) Why were tensions high between the United States and Japan by 1940? _The United States and many European countries enacted high protective tariffs that stifled Japanese exports and increased Japan's poor economic condition. President Roosevelt decided not to renew the 1911 U.S.-Japan Treaty of Commerce and Navigation in July 1939. Then the U.S. Congress passed the Export Control Act in July 1940. These two actions eliminated Japan's primary source of oil, scrap metal and other material resources needed for war._ (Page 11)

3) What kind of military presence was in Alaska before the bombing of Pearl Harbor? _As tensions between Japan and the United States grew, a significant military presence started building in Alaska. Construction of naval stations at Kodiak and Dutch Harbor began, the Naval Air Station at Sitka was expanded, and work started in June 1940 on building Fort Richardson and Elmendorf Field, near Anchorage. And although construction of Ladd Field, east of Fairbanks, began in the fall of 1938, it welcomed its first U.S. Army Air Corps troops in spring 1940._ (Page 12)

4) Explain the Lend-Lease Act. _In March 1941, the Lend-Lease Act empowered the president to give aid to friendly nations in exchange for whatever kind of compensation or benefit he thought acceptable. Aid ranged from heavy war material and munitions to industrial equipment, raw material, agricultural products and many other items._ (Page 13)

5) How did the United States benefit from the Lend-Lease Act after Japan attacked Pearl Harbor? *Four days after the Japanese attack on Pearl Harbor on Dec. 7, 1941, Nazi Germany declared war on the United States. Following its declaration of war, the United States and 14 of its allies signed lend-lease agreements. Between 1941-1945, the U.S. gave its allies $50 billion in military aid. In return, America benefited from reciprocal aid, such as rental of military bases on Allied soil, the pooling of resources and manpower, and the inventive genius of every Allied power toward winning the war.* (Page 13)

DISCUSSION QUESTION

(Discuss this question with your teacher or write your answer in essay form below. Use additional paper if necessary.)

Why did the Army close all of its forts in Alaska between 1921-1925?

ENRICHMENT ACTIVITY

Read eyewitness accounts from Pearl Harbor by visiting the link below. Next, it is your turn to interview an older relative or community member about their memories of Pearl Harbor. Write down at least three questions to ask during your interview. http://teacher.scholastic.com/pearl/eyewits.htm

LEARN MORE

Learn more about the attack on Pearl Harbor by visiting https://www.history.navy.mil/browse-by-topic/wars-conflicts-and-operations/world-war-ii/1941/pearl-harbor.html

UNIT 1: WORLD WAR II ERUPTS
LESSON 2: RUSSIA'S SECRET MISSION

FACTS TO KNOW

    Ladd Field – Alaska's first airfield, named after Maj. Arthur Ladd who was killed in a plane crash in South Carolina in 1935
    Soviet – A citizen and/or soldier of the former Union of Soviet Socialist Republics
    Henry H. Arnold – Commander of U.S. Army Air Forces who recommended that an air base be built at Fairbanks

COMPREHENSION QUESTIONS

1) Why was a stronger military presence in Alaska important to America's defense? _Prior to Ladd's opening in 1940, Alaska was a vast, undefended territory. The only active military installation was the Chilkoot Barracks, located in Haines. There were no military airfields. Military leaders and government officials believed that Alaska's location was a strategic location for America's military defense._ (Pages 15-17)

2) What part did Henry Arnold play in increasing military presence in Alaska? _U.S. Army Air Forces Commander Henry H. "Hap" Arnold recommended that an air base be built at Fairbanks that could support cold weather testing and serve as a tactical supply depot. He pressured Congress for funds until the military received $4 million to build the airfield, and in August 1939, surveyors arrived and got the project under way._ (Pages 16-17)

3) What was the cold weather experimental station? _The cold weather experimental station focused on developing standards for servicing and operating planes in subzero temperatures, testing a multitude of aircraft parts and analyzing arctic operations that included communications equipment, medical issues and survival gear._ (Page 19)

4) What secret mission made Ladd Field a vital link between America and the Soviet Union? _In the fall of 1942, the United States and the Soviet Union signed a lend-lease agreement that made Ladd Field a vital link in a secret mission to get American-made aircraft to the Russian front. Ladd became the official aircraft transfer point between the two nations._ (Page 19)

5) What was life like for Russian soldiers at Ladd Field? *The base provided the Soviets with food, sleeping quarters and hangar space. When it came to flying, the Russians always led the field and were given priority for takeoff, according to Otis Hays Jr. in The Alaska-Siberian Connection: The World War II Air Route. But the officers' mess was a different story. "We took the first time that was most convenient to us," pilot Randy Acord later recalled, "and then the Russians would have to fit into that. Russian officers also could buy things at the Base Exchange and arrange for the use of motor vehicles with American drivers.* (Pages 22-24)

DISCUSSION QUESTION

(Discuss this question with your teacher or write your answer in essay form below. Use additional paper if necessary.)

Why did Russia want to keep the Lend-Lease Agreement with the United States a secret?

ENRICHMENT ACTIVITY

Take some time to show your appreciation to those who risk their lives to protect our country.

Note to teacher: Visit the link below. Choose one project to do as a class or invite students to choose individual projects from the list.

https://service-project-ideas.jimdo.com/service-project-ideas/military-veterans/

LEARN MORE

Read more about the long history of Ladd Field by visiting https://www.army.mil/article/41754/ladd-field-has-long-history/

UNIT 1: WORLD WAR II ERUPTS

LESSON 3: ARMY BASE REVITALIZES ANCHORAGE

FACTS TO KNOW

Fort Richardson – The first Army base in Anchorage built in 1940; later named Elmendorf Air Force Base (recently renamed again to Joint Base Elmendorf-Richardson – called J-BER)
Col. Simon Bolivar Buckner – Led the Alaska Defense Force in Anchorage

COMPREHENSION QUESTIONS

1) What was Anchorage like before the military began building Fort Richardson in 1940? *Before the military began building the original Fort Richardson in 1940, which later became Elmendorf Air Force Base, Anchorage was a typical small town. In 1938, the city's 4,000 residents had no paved roads, no street or traffic lights and the police chief clocked speeders by using his stopwatch. (Pages 27-28)*

2) What issues did Anchorage face with the large stream of workers coming in to work on the army base? *With the population surge, housing became a major problem. "Construction workers walked the streets at night and many spread blankets and slept on the ground," wrote Elizabeth Tower in Anchorage, part of the City History Series. "Families remodeled garages or built tar-paper shacks on the back of their lots and rented them at fantastic prices." (Pages 29-30)*

3) What monumental task did Col. Simon Buckner face? *Col. Simon Bolivar Buckner Jr. assumed command of the newly created Alaska Defense Force. Buckner faced a monumental task, as Alaska had no airfields suitable for military aircraft and no land routes to connect it with the Continental United States. Other than Ladd Army Airfield, which was under construction, the only other Army installation in the Last Frontier was the Chilkoot Barracks in Haines. (Pages 32-33)*

4) Why was construction of Fort Richardson slow? *Workers encountered muskeg, a compilation of small plants, moss and roots that went down several feet. The spongy surface had to be pealed back until crews found a solid surface, like bedrock, on which to build. Equipment, in short supply, often got stuck in the muck. And while local resources, particularly lumber, were used whenever possible, nearly all equipment, parts and food had to come by ship from the Lower 48. (Page 33)*

5) How did life change for Alaskan's after the attack on Pearl Harbor in 1941?
Residents had to tape dark shades on their windows at night or paint their windows black – leaving tiny slits in the middle for sunlight to enter. Any light that escaped could signal disaster. Streetlights were turned off, and cars drove through the winter darkness with only parking lights to illuminate the way. Trenches also were dug to protect Anchorage citizens in the event of Japanese air attacks. When sirens sounded, residents were to leave their homes and hide in the trenches. (Pages 35-36)

DISCUSSION QUESTION

(Discuss this question with your teacher or write your answer in essay form below. Use additional paper if necessary.)

How did Fort Richardson "revitalize" Anchorage?

_____
_____
_____
_____
_____
_____
_____
_____
_____
_____
_____
_____
_____
_____
_____
_____
_____
_____

LEARN MORE

Read more about the military history of Alaska by visiting:
http://www.akhistorycourse.org/alaskas-cultures/military-in-alaska

TIME TO REVIEW

Review Chapters 1-3 of your book before moving on the Unit Review. See how many questions you can answer without looking at your book.

UNIT 1: WORLD WAR II ERUPTS

REVIEW LESSONS 1-3

Write down what you remember about:

Pearl Harbor – <u>Hawaiian port that was attacked with bombs by Japan on December 7, 1941</u>

President Franklin D. Roosevelt – <u>The 32nd president of the United States who declared war on Japan after the bombing of Pearl Harbor</u>

Ladd Field – <u>Alaska's first airfield named after Maj. Arthur Ladd who was killed in a plane crash in South Carolina in 1935</u>

Soviet – <u>A citizen and/or soldier of the former Union of Soviet Socialist Republics</u>

Henry H. Arnold – <u>Commander of U.S. Army Air Forces who recommended that an air base be built at Fairbanks</u>

Fort Richardson – <u>The first Army base in Anchorage built in 1940; later named Elmendorf Air Force Base (recently renamed again to Joint Base Elmendorf-Richardson – called J-BER)</u>

Col. Simon Bolivar Buckner – <u>Led the Alaska Defense Force in Anchorage</u>

Fill in the blanks:

1) On December <u>8, 1941</u>, one day after the early morning attack on <u>Pearl Harbor</u>, U.S. President <u>Franklin D. Roosevelt</u> went before both houses of Congress to request a declaration of war against <u>Japan</u>.

2) "If we would provide an adequate <u>defense</u> for the United States, we must have <u>Alaska</u> to dominate the North Pacific," said U.S. Secretary of State <u>William Seward</u> in a speech to convince Congress of the value of buying <u>Alaska</u> in the mid-1860s.

3) Prior to the opening of *Ladd Field* in 1940, Alaska was a vast, undefended territory. The only active military installation was the *Chilkoot Barracks*, located in Haines. There were no military *airfields.*

4) In the fall of 1942, the United States and the *Soviet Union* signed a *lend-lease* agreement that made *Ladd Field* a vital link in a secret mission to get American-made *aircraft* to the *Russian* front. *Ladd* Field became the official *aircraft* transfer point between the two nations.

5) The Americans wanted to fly the planes on to Siberia, but *Russian* leader *Joseph Stalin* said no. He didn't want any appearance of *U.S.-Soviet* collaboration in the Far East, as his country and *Japan* were not at war and he wanted to avoid any incidents that might incite the *Japanese.*

6) Before the military began building the original *Fort Richardson* in 1940, which later became *Elmendorf Air* Force Base, *Anchorage* was a typical small town. In 1938, the city's 4,000 residents had no *paved* roads, no street or *traffic* lights and the police chief *clocked speeders* by using his stopwatch.

7) Congress finally realized that *Russia*, at the time an ally of Germany, only lay *55* miles away from Alaska at the point where the *Seward* Peninsula and the *Chukotka* Peninsula reach out toward each other.

8) Following the attack on *Pearl Harbor* by *Japan* on Dec. 7, 1941, progress on the base's construction ramped up and life changed dramatically for Alaskans. Residents had to tape *dark shades on their windows* at night or *paint* their windows black. *Streetlights* were turned off, and cars drove through the winter darkness with only parking lights to illuminate the way. When *sirens* sounded, residents were to leave their homes and hide in the *trenches.*

Alaska & World War II
Word Scramble Puzzle Key
Unscramble the words below

#	Scrambled	Answer	Clue
1.	prlae rboarh	pearl harbor	U.S. President Franklin D. Roosevelt declared war on Japan after it bombed this location
2.	khlooitc	chilkoot	Only military barracks in Alaska when United States entered World War II
3.	iaskt	sitka	In 1937, the U.S. Navy established a small seaplane base at this Southeast town
4.	hcdnsirora	richardson	The U.S. Army began building this military base near Anchorage in 1940
5.	addl	ladd	This cold-weather experimental station in Fairbanks welcomed its first U.S. Army Air Corps troops in 1940
6.	isrnusa	**russian**	American military turned airplanes over to these pilots in Fairbanks in lend-lease program
7.	cceletri uwaeerrdn	electric underwear	Development of these at cold-weather experimental station was a hit with aviators
8.	cknrbeu	buckner	This military officer took command of the Alaska Defense Force
9.	feneodlrm	elmendorf	Name of military airfield created near Anchorage
10.	**evere**	reeve	Alaska bush pilot who flew more than 1,100 tons of equipment and 300 men from Anchorage to military sites in 1941

UNIT 1: WORLD WAR II ERUPTS

UNIT TEST

Choose *two* of the following questions to answer in paragraph form. Use as much detail as possible to completely answer the question.

1) What major event in U.S. history caused the government to push for stronger military presence in Alaska? How did this event change everyday life for Alaskans?

2) Describe the secret mission between America and Russia. Why was this mission kept secret?

3) Why was Alaska an ideal location for a U.S. Army base? In what city did the military build an Army base in 1940? How did the Army base revitalize this city?

TEACHER NOTES ABOUT THIS UNIT

UNIT 2: MILITARY ROUTES EMERGE

LESSON 4: RAILROADER TUNNELS TO WHITTIER

FACTS TO KNOW

Whittier – A city at the head of the Passage Canal in the U.S. state of Alaska, southeast of Anchorage

Anton Anderson – Engineered the Anton Anderson Tunnel into Whittier

COMPREHENSION QUESTIONS

1) What was the purpose of building a railroad spur from Anchorage to Whittier? *The project was initiated because of a concern that the long railroad route to Seward, particularly the Loop District with its trestles, was vulnerable to attack by Japanese bombers. Military leaders wanted to provide the Anchorage base with a safer link to a deep-water port that would protect their main supply line. (Page 40)*

2) Who oversaw the railroad project? What experience did this man have in railroad building? *Anton Anderson. Anderson had vast experience in railroad building in the Last Frontier. He had labored as a railroader along with many hardy men after the U.S. government chose Seward as the saltwater terminus for its proposed railroad in 1915. Anderson worked as an axman on a survey party for the Alaska Road Commission. Through his work, he was instrumental in the development of Western Alaska and surveyed and engineered much of the railroad line. (Pages 40-42)*

3) What was the tunnel engineer's nickname? Why? What did he consider his greatest accomplishment? *On May 24, 1917, Anderson started working as an axman on a survey party for the Alaska Road Commission. That date began a long and distinguished career that led the native New Zealander into public service and earned him the title "Mr. Alaska Railroad." He considered the construction of the Whittier railroad tunnel his greatest achievement. (Page 42)*

4) As the War Department studied possible railroad routes, why did they choose the Passage Canal Line? *The military needed a secure transportation system for troops, equipment and supplies, and a War Department study in 1940 concluded that the Passage Canal line would be safer from enemy attack than the Seward line. President Franklin D. Roosevelt approved the spur to Whittier in April 1941. (Page 43)*

5) Describe how the Anton Anderson Tunnel was constructed.

Workers drilled from both ends of the mountain, part of the Chugach Range, toward each other. In November 1942, the two crews met in the middle. By June 1943, workers completed laying track over the 14-mile route and the first trains rolled through the Anton Anderson Tunnel into Whittier. (Page 45)

DISCUSSION QUESTION

(Discuss this question with your teacher or write your answer in essay form below. Use additional paper if necessary.)

What joke did the drilling crew play on Anton Anderson?

_____
_____
_____
_____
_____
_____
_____
_____
_____
_____
_____
_____
_____
_____
_____
_____
_____

ENRICHMENT ACTIVITY

Imagine that you are a news reporter covering the construction of the Anton Anderson Tunnel. Write out a live scene using the information that you learned in Chapter 4.

LEARN MORE

Read more about the Anton Anderson Memorial Tunnel by visiting http://www.tunnel.alaska.gov/history.shtml

UNIT 2: MILITARY ROUTES EMERGE

LESSON 5: ROAD HEADS NORTH TO ALASKA
LESSON 6: OUTPOSTS SPROUT UP

Note: Read both chapters 5 and 6 before completing this lesson.

FACTS TO KNOW

Alaska-Canada Highway – Major highway built to connect Alaska to the Continentual United States and stretched 1,422 miles from Dawson Creek, British Columbia, to Delta Junction, Alaska

Donald MacDonald – Engineer who worked with Clyde Williams to push Congress to build the Alaska-Canada Highway

Clyde "Slim" Williams – Alaska-Canada Highway advocate who traveled the route several times to gain support to build it

COMPREHENSION QUESTIONS

1) What was Donald MacDonald's dream? *Donald MacDonald, a locating engineer with the Alaska Road Commission, had dreamed for years of an overland coastal route to Alaska. It would run north from Seattle across British Columbia through the Yukon Territory to Fairbanks. (Page 48)*

2) Why did Clyde Williams travel by dog sled to Chicago? *In the early 1930s, MacDonald heard about a Copper Center man who had boasted that he and his dog team could make it to Chicago over prospector trails. So MacDonald contacted Clyde "Slim" Williams and convinced the 50-year-old trapper to prove it. (Pages 48-49)*

3) Why did Clyde Williams go to Washington D.C. after his trip to Chicago? *Williams and his dog team mushed on to Washington, D.C., where they camped in a city park and met with Alaska's Delegate, Anthony J. Dimond, and other members of Congress. He also briefed President Franklin D. Roosevelt on the proposal for a road. Years later, Eleanor Roosevelt would say that Williams was a most vocal advocate for the Alaska Highway. (Page 49)*

4) How did Clyde Williams and his friend John Logan become the first men to travel by motorcycle from Alaska to Seattle?
Williams again made a trip south in 1939 to gain support for the highway. He and adventurer John Logan, along with Siberian husky Blizzard, left Fairbanks on May 14 on board specially modified British-made motorcycles. The men headed down the same route Williams had traveled a few years earlier. (Pages 250-251)

5) How did the bombing of Pearl Harbor influence the building of the highway? *Following the attack, American officials realized that Alaska was vulnerable to Japanese invasion – especially with only 750 miles separating the last island in the Aleutian Chain and the nearest Japanese military base. The need for more military in Alaska became urgent, and a road to transport troops, equipment and supplies became a priority.* (Pages 52-53)

6) How did a group of more than 3,000 African-American soldiers who took part in building the Alaska-Canada highway change the perceptions of the time? *Many in the military thought black engineers were not as skilled and industrious as Caucasians. African-American and white units had been kept separate since the Civil War. But the black troops sent to build the highway changed many people's minds. The hard-working men worked shoulder to shoulder to help build hundreds of miles of road through densely forested land in just eight months. Their contribution to the road effort helped change the situation for African-Americans in the military – which desegregated in 1948.* (Pages 55-56)

7) What kind of conditions did the workers face while building the Alaska-Canada Highway? *All the troops worked through temperatures exceeding 50 degrees below zero during the winter months. In June, they suffered through constant rain that turned the sodden ground into a quagmire that grabbed vehicles and held them by the hubcaps. They then labored night and day during the summer, when the sun provided more than 20 hours of light and temperatures rose to 90 degrees above zero.* (Pages 56-57)

8) Name three military outposts that you read about in Chapter 6 and one fact about each. *Answers to this question will vary.* (Pages 73-93)

DISCUSSION QUESTION

(Discuss this question with your teacher or write your answer in essay form below. Use additional paper if necessary.)

How did the building of railroads, highways and military outposts change the population of many Alaskan cities?

_____
_____
_____
_____
_____
_____
_____
_____
_____
_____
_____
_____
_____
_____
_____
_____
_____
_____

LEARN MORE

Read more about road transportation in Alaska by visiting http://www.akhistorycourse.org/americas-territory/alaskas-heritage/chapter-4-10-road-transportation

MAP ACTIVITY

Trace the Alaska-Canada Highway on the map below. Mark the major centers that the highway runs through from Dawson Creek in Canada to Delta Junction in Alaska.

1) Fort St. John   2) Fort Nelson   3) Muncho Lake   4) Watson Lake
5) Teslin Lake   6) Whitehorse   7) Tok

UNIT 3: A FEW GOOD MEN

LESSON 7: ESKIMO SCOUTS VOLUNTEER

FACTS TO KNOW

    Alaska Territorial Guard – Military unit made up of Native Alaskans to protect the territory from Japanese invaders

    U.S. Army Maj. Marvin R. Marston – One of the commanders of the Alaska Territorial Guard who also helped to develop it

    Territorial Gov. Ernest Gruening – Authorized the creation of the Alaska Territorial Guard

COMPREHENSION QUESTIONS

1) How did Maj. Marvin Marston get the idea of an Alaska Native defense force?
U.S. Army Maj. Marvin R. Marston conceived the idea of an Alaska Native defense force after visiting St. Lawrence Island on a military morale-boosting trip with comedian Joe E. Brown. After Marston learned that a crew from a Japanese vessel had recently come ashore and spent several days on the island, he thought about setting up defense units comprised of Alaska Natives throughout western Alaska. (Page 95)

2) Why was Territorial Gov. Ernest Gruening supportive of the idea when many were not? *Following the bombing of Pearl Harbor, the Alaska National Guard was federalized and became the 297th Infantry. Other available men had been drafted overseas. That left the 586,000-squaremile territory, whose military bases were still under construction, unprotected. The governor wanted a local guard. (Pages 95-96)*

3) What reservations did Gov. Gruening have about enlisting Native People into the Alaska Territorial Guard? *He had little firsthand experience with them but had read how they had been affected negatively by the intrusion of white men into their land – including depletion of their food supply, decimation by diseases and taken advantage of due to their naiveté. He wondered if they resented White people and held deep-seated resentments. (Pages 96-97)*

4) According to Maj. Marston, how could the Native people help protect Alaska?
"We need you to be the eyes and ears of the Army," he said. "You know how to hunt the seal and the walrus. You're fine shots. I want every man who is willing to join the Alaska Territorial Guard." Marston's speeches to the people usually ended with the same statement. "We will give you guns and ammunition. If the Japanese comes here, and

lands his boat, will you shoot him quick? You men who will help your country against the Japanese, come forward now and sign your names here on this paper." (Page 99)

5) When was the territorial guard disbanded? When was the unit officially recognized as military veterans? *Alaska disbanded the Territorial Guard in 1947, with no fanfare for the volunteers who proudly wore World War I-era uniforms bearing a blue patch embroidered with gold stars of the Big Dipper and the letters ATG. It wasn't until 2004 that the Alaska unit was officially recognized as military veterans. (Pages 101-102)*

DISCUSSION QUESTION

(Discuss this question with your teacher or write your answer in essay form below. Use additional paper if necessary.)

Why do you think the Native people of Alaska were so eager to join the Alaska Territorial Guard?

_____
_____
_____
_____
_____
_____
_____
_____
_____
_____
_____
_____
_____
_____
_____
_____
_____

ENRICHMENT ACTIVITY

Watch this short YouTube video to see some of the faces of people who served in the Alaska Territorial Guard https://www.youtube.com/watch?v=JEU3y5vH_sk

LEARN MORE

Men of the Tundra: Eskimos at War, By Marvin A. Marston. New York: October House, 1969.

This World War II poster depicts the Alaska Territorial Guard

UNIT 3: A FEW GOOD MEN

LESSON 8: THE FLYING BARITONE FROM FAIRBANKS

FACTS TO KNOW

Robert MacArthur Crawford – Composer of the Official U.S. Air Force Song
Composer – A person who writes a song

COMPREHENSION QUESTIONS

1) How did Robert MacArthur Crawford begin his music career in Alaska? *Robert Crawford spent his youth in Fairbanks singing for early settlers in the northern gold-rush town. Bob ordered an instrument from a mail-order house, but under the teaching of Fairbanks' musician Vic Durand, he turned his attention to the piano and composing. (Pages 106-107)*

2) At which prestigious U.S. university did Crawford study? What organization did he start while studying there? What did he do upon graduation? *While studying at Princeton, he also took part in many extracurricular activities and started the Princeton University Orchestra. For seven years, he directed and orchestrated the music of the annual Triangle Show. Following graduation, he won a scholarship to the school of Conservatoire American at Fontainebleau in France. (Page 107)*

3) Besides music, what was Robert MacArthur Crawford's passion? How did he blend his two passions to win a contest? *The young musician developed another passion during this time – aviation. Crawford's love for flying and the wild, blue yonder prompted him to enter a contest to find a song for the U.S. Army Air Corps. Just before the July 1939 deadline, Crawford entered his song. It fit the bill, and the committee unanimously voted it as the winner. (Pages 108-109)*

4) What award did he win in 1965 and why? *In 1965, an Air Force Scroll of Appreciation was awarded to Crawford – the first official recognition by the Air Force of the writer of the famed flying song. It was awarded posthumously, for Crawford had died on March 12, 1961, in New York City. His widow, Hester, accepted it on his behalf. (Page 110)*

DISCUSSION QUESTION

(Discuss this question with your teacher or write your answer in essay form below. Use additional paper if necessary.)

Why do you think his nickname was the "Flying Baritone"?

_____
_____
_____
_____
_____
_____
_____
_____
_____
_____
_____
_____
_____
_____
_____
_____
_____
_____

ENRICHMENT ACTIVITY

Watch this short YouTube video to hear Robert MacArthur Crawford's famous song: https://www.youtube.com/watch?v=8B7RzQftARE

LEARN MORE

Read more about John MacArthur Crawford by visiting http://www.militarynews.com/peninsula-warrior/features/army_features/behind-the-name-crawford-hall-named-for-father-of-the/article_ec5dd9c4-2796-57a0-bce7-6a9865b37a0c.html

UNIT 3: A FEW GOOD MEN

LESSON 9: J. DOOLITTLE: NOME TOWN BOY

FACTS TO KNOW

Jimmy Doolittle – Leader of the famous Doolittle Raiders that bombed Tokyo in 1942
Nome – Gold-rush town located on the southern Seward Peninsula coast on Norton Sound

COMPREHENSION QUESTIONS

1) What was life like for Jimmy Doolittle growing up in Nome in the early 1900s? *His father came to Nome to look for gold. It was one of the most lawless mining camps in the world. It was the paradise of thieves, thugs, cheats, outlaws and the most degraded type of sporting women and their parasites, according to reports at the time. The other boys made fun of his long girl-like curls. (Pages 113-115)*

2) What lesson did Jimmy Doolittle learn at an early age? What medical condition was he diagnosed with, and what was the cause of it? *With many fights to his credit, he learned early in life to take care of himself. When he learned that dog-team drivers and runners were looked up to in gold-rush Nome, he decided to be a runner, since he didn't have any dogs. And he'd run until he collapsed. Years later, doctors diagnosed a heart murmur deemed caused by over-exertion when he was young. (Page 115)*

3) When Jimmy and his mother moved to Los Angeles after his father's death, what did he become known for? *While Jimmy and his mother made Los Angeles their home, the small boy continued his scrappy ways and became known for his ability as a fighter. He learned how to box and became amateur bantamweight champion of the West Coast in 1912 at age 15. (Page 116)*

4) When did he become interested in aviation? Name some of his accomplishments as an aviator for the military. *When Jimmy saw his first airplane in Los Angeles, he became interested in aviation. When World War I came along in 1917, Jimmy enlisted in the Signal Corps Reserve, Aviation Section. He set a record for crossing the continent in 1922, acquired one of the first doctoral degrees in aeronautical engineering and won the coveted Schneider trophy, the Harmon trophy and the Bendix trophy. (Pages 116-117)*

5) What was the pinnacle of his career? Why was this event important in World War II?
He was the leader of the famous raiders that took off from the aircraft carrier Hornet and successfully bombed Tokyo on April 18, 1942. The Doolittle Raid is viewed by historians as a major morale-building victory for the United States. The raid showed the Japanese that their homeland was vulnerable to air attack and forced them to withdraw several frontline fighter units from Pacific war zones for homeland defense. Their attempt to close the perceived gap in their Pacific defense perimeter led directly to the decisive American victory during the Battle of Midway in June 1942. (Pages 117-119)

DISCUSSION QUESTION

(Discuss this question with your teacher or write your answer in essay form below. Use additional paper if necessary.)

Do you think that Jimmy Doolittle's childhood experiences prepared him for all the major accomplishments he had as an aviator? Explain your answer.

_____
_____
_____
_____
_____
_____
_____
_____
_____
_____
_____
_____
_____
_____
_____
_____
_____

TIME TO REVIEW

Review Chapters 4-9 of your book before moving on the Unit Review. See how many questions you can answer without looking at your book.

Courtesy U.S. Air Force

On April 18, 1942, airmen of the U.S. Army Air Forces, led by Lt. Col. James H. (Jimmy) Doolittle, carried the Battle of the Pacific to the heart of the Japanese empire with a surprising and daring raid on military targets at Tokyo, Yokohama, Yokosuka, Nagoya and Kobe. This heroic attack against these major cities was the result of coordination between the Army Air Forces and the U.S. Navy, which carried 16 North American B-25 medium bombers aboard the carrier *USS Hornet* to within take-off distance of the Japanese Islands.

The Japanese thought the airplanes had taken off from a base in the Aleutian Chain of Alaska, which is one reason why they bombed Dutch Harbor, Attu and Kiska in June 1942.

Source: National Museum of the U.S. Air Force

UNIT 2: MILITARY ROUTES EMERGE
UNIT 3: A FEW GOOD MEN

REVIEW LESSONS 4-9

Write down what you remember about:

Whittier – *A city at the head of the Passage Canal in the U.S. state of Alaska, about 58 miles southeast of Anchorage*

Anton Anderson – *Engineered the Anton Anderson Tunnel into Whittier*

Alaska-Canada Highway – *Major highway built to connect Alaska to the Continentual United States and stretched 1,422 miles from Dawson Creek, British Columbia, to Delta Junction, Alaska*

Donald MacDonald – *Engineer who worked with Clyde Williams to push Congress to build the Alaska-Canada Highway*

Clyde "Slim" Williams – *Alaska-Canada highway advocate who traveled the route several times to gain support to build it*

Alaska Territorial Guard – *Military unit made up of Native Alaskans to protect the territory from Japanese invaders*

U.S. Army Maj. Marvin R. Marston – *One of the commanders of the Alaska Territorial Guard who also helped to develop it*

Territorial Gov. Ernest Gruening – *Authorized the Alaska Territorial Guard*

Robert MacArthur Crawford – *Composer of the Official U.S. Air Force Song*

Composer – *A person who writes a song*

Jimmy Doolittle – *Leader of the famous Doolittle Raiders that bombed Tokyo in 1942*

Nome – *Gold-rush town located on the southern Seward Peninsula coast on Norton Sound*

Fill in the blanks:

1) *Anton Anderson* engineered the project that pierced through three miles of solid *granite* to open the Port of *Whittier* to the Railbelt and to Fort *Richardson*, 75 miles away.

2) The *military* needed a secure transportation system for *troops, equipment and supplies*, and a War Department study in 1940 concluded that the *Passage* Canal line would be safer from enemy attack than the *Seward* line.

3) Called one of America's greatest *construction* projects, the *Alaska-Canada* Highway stretched 1,422 miles from *Dawson Creek, British Columbia*, to *Delta Junction*, Alaska.

4) In the early 1930s, *Donald MacDonald* heard about a Copper Center man who had boasted that he and his *dog team* could make it to *Chicago* over prospector trails. So *MacDonald* contacted *Clyde "Slim" Williams* and convinced the 50-year-old trapper to prove it.

5) With the bombing of *Pearl Harbor* by the *Japanese* on Dec. 7, 1941, the need for more military in Alaska became urgent, and a road to transport *troops, equipment and supplies* became a priority. American officials realized that Alaska was vulnerable to *Japanese invasion* – especially with only 750 miles separating the last island in the *Aleutian* Chain and the nearest *Japanese* military base.

6) U.S. Army Maj. *Marvin R. Marston* conceived the idea of an *Alaska Native* defense force after visiting *St. Lawrence* Island. While on the island, *Marston* noted that all the white men, except for a school teacher, had left and that the 700 Natives living in the island's two villages of Savoonga and Gambell were nervous about *possible occupation by Japanese forces*.

7) Territorial Gov. *Ernest Gruening* said the response of the *white* men and *Native* men differed when asked to join the *territorial* guard. "In various communities *white* men asked *how much they would be paid*," *Gruening* said. "My reply was that they would be *paid nothing*. They would have the privilege of defending their homes and their families if the enemy should come. No *Eskimos* ever raised that question.

8) *Robert MacArthur Crawford* began his musical career by singing for miners in early *Fairbanks*. His musical *composition* ability soon became evident when he wrote the words and music for a song titled "*My Northland*."

9) *Crawford's* love for *flying* and the wild, blue yonder prompted him to enter a contest to find a *song* for the U.S. Army Air Corps. *Crawford*, known by now as the "*Flying Baritone*," was handed the $1,000 first-place prize at the 1939 National Air races in Cleveland, Ohio.

10) "*Nome Town Boy Makes Good*" proclaimed the Nome Nugget headline in April 1942. One of Nome's own, U.S. Army Air Forces pilot Lt. Col. *James Doolittle*, had led the *Tokyo bombing* raid in World War *II*.

11) With many *fights* to his credit, he learned early in life to take care of himself. When he learned that *dog-team drivers and runners* were looked up to in gold-rush Nome, *Jimmy Doolittle* decided to be a *runner*, since he didn't have any dogs. Years later, doctors diagnosed a *heart murmur* deemed caused by over-exertion when he was young.

12) The raid showed the *Japanese* that their homeland was vulnerable to *air attack* and forced them to withdraw several frontline fighter units from *Pacific* war zones for homeland defense. Their attempt to close the perceived gap in their *Pacific* defense perimeter led directly to the decisive *American* victory during the Battle of Midway in June 1942.

The Alaska Territorial Guard, also known as the Eskimo Scouts, played a large role in the protection of Alaska from Japanese forces. Here the Guard marches up Main Street toward St. Michael's Russian Orthodox Church in Sitka in 1944.

World War II Routes & Men
Crossword Puzzle

Read Across and Down clues and fill in blank boxes that match numbers on the clues

Across
6   Alaska governor who authorized the creation of the Alaska Territorial Guard
7   Groups of soldiers
11 Clyde Williams' dogs were part this animal
13 Point in Canada where Alaska-Canada Highway began during WWII
15 Nickname of Clyde Williams
17 Man who led air raid on Tokyo in 1942
20 This Roosevelt said Clyde Williams was "a most vocal advocate" for Alaska Highway
23 Place where military held official ceremony of Alaska Highway completion on Nov. 20, 1942
25 Uninhabited region
26 The man who engineered the railroad tunnel through Maynard Mountain
27 Structures that span rivers and streams
31 Man who wrote and composed the official U.S. Air Force song
32 Alaska Natives signed up to guard Alaska's coasts and became known as this
33 Number of stanzas in the official U.S. Air Force song
34 The practice of keeping White troops and African-American troops separated

Down
1   Man who conceived the idea for an Alaska Native defense force
2   How the military hid the Jesse Lee Home complex in Seward from enemy eyes
3   Alaska's delegate to Congress in 1933
4   Material used to create runways on Alaska islands
5   Pesky insects that suck blood and bothered the workers on the Alaska Highway
8   Only American military aircraft named after a specific person
9   Route that U.S. and Canada chose to build the Alaska-Canada highway in 1942
10 Type of wheels that Clyde Williams put on his sled to mush to Lower 48
11 Port at the end of the railroad spur from Anchorage that military needed for transporting troops and supplies during WWII
12 A powertul tractor with a broad upright blade at the front for clearing ground
14 Military's cold-weather experimental station in Fairbanks
16 Name of Clyde Williams' dog
18 Point in Alaska where Alaska-Canada Highway ended during WWII
19 The nickname for the man who organized the Alaska Natives for the Alaska Territorial Guard
21 Nickname for the Alaska-Canada Highway
22 A person who works for the railroad
24 Means of transportation for William's 1939 trip to Seattle

World War II Routes & Men
Crossword Puzzle Key

Down (Continued)
28 Town where Clyde Williams mushed for World's Fair in 1933
29 U.S. declared war against this country on Dec. 8, 1941
30 A large woodland

UNIT 2: MILITARY ROUTES EMERGE
UNIT 3: A FEW GOOD MEN

UNIT TEST

Choose *three* of the following questions to answer in paragraph form. Use as much detail as possible to completely answer the question.

1) What was the purpose of the Anton Anderson Tunnel? How was it built? Why was this location chosen?

2) Describe the conditions that the construction workers faced building the Alaska-Canada Highway. How did a unit of over 3,000 African-American construction workers change the perceptions of the day?

3) Why did Maj. Marvin Marston think that it would be a good idea to organize an Alaska Native defense force? How did the Native people of Alaska react to the invitation to join the unit? Why?

4) Who was the "Flying Baritone"? How did he begin his musical career? What song was he most famous for? Why was this song so popular?

5) How did Jimmy Doolittle's childhood impact his career as an adult? What were some of his accomplishments? How did his most famous accomplishment change World War II?

TEACHER NOTES ABOUT THIS UNIT

TEACHER NOTES ABOUT THIS UNIT

UNIT 4: CONFLICT IN THE ALEUTIANS

LESSON 10: DUTCH HARBOR ATTACKED

FACTS TO KNOW

    Dutch Harbor – Area on Unalaska Island that was attacked by Japanese troops in 1942

    Japanese Zeros – Fighter aircraft also known as Mitsubishi A6M or Navy Type 0

    Code breakers – Military personnel trained to interpret encrypted messages

COMPREHENSION QUESTIONS

1) What happened during the two-day attack on Dutch Harbor in 1942?
Japanese soldiers invaded the Aleutian Islands on June 3, 1942. U.S. forces at Fort Mears at Dutch Harbor met the attack with anti-aircraft and small arms fire. They downed two Japanese planes. Another attack at 9 a.m. targeted five U.S. destroyers sighted by a Japanese fighter plane on the first attack. On June 4, nine Japanese fighters and 17 bombers again struck Dutch Harbor, located on Unalaska Island. (Pages 120-121)

2) How many Americans died in the attack? Explain how it could have been worse.
During the two-day attack, 33 U.S. soldiers and sailors, as well as 10 civilians, died. Rear Adm. Kakuji Kakuta had dispatched more than 30 planes from two small aircraft carriers, the Ryujo and Junyo, hidden in the waters off Unalaska. Due to fog, high seas and strong winds, less than half the planes reached the island. (Page 121)

3) What misconceptions did the Japanese planners have about American military support in the region?
The Imperial High Command thought the American raid had started out from a secret base in the western Aleutians. Japanese planners also thought the United States had extensive military installations at Dutch Harbor and smaller garrisons on Adak, Kiska and Attu. The Americans actually had little military support in the Aleutians at the time of the attack. (Page 125)

4) How did code breakers help American soldiers learn about the Japanese plan of attack?
American code breakers learned in mid-March that the Japanese planned to bomb, and then occupy, the Aleutians. The decoded messages also revealed that the main thrust of the Japanese attack would be Midway, so that's where the Americans sent the majority of its fleet. Intercepts in May pinpointed Dutch Harbor as the main target in the Aleutians. (Page 125)

5) How did American soldiers respond to these plans?
The U.S. military responded quickly and moved planes forward to the new Alaska Peninsula air bases, where supplies of gasoline and bombs had been stockpiled. By June 1, 1942, one heavy and six medium bombers and 17 fighter planes were sitting on Umnak and six bombers and 16 fighters at Cold Bay. The Navy also reacted to the threat of a Japanese attack, placing five cruisers, 14 destroyers and six submarines off Kodiak. (Page 126)

DISCUSSION QUESTION

(Discuss this question with your teacher or write your answer in essay form below. Use additional paper if necessary.)

Do you think the Japanese attack on Dutch Harbor changed Alaska? Explain your answer.

_____
_____
_____
_____
_____
_____
_____
_____
_____
_____
_____
_____
_____
_____
_____
_____
_____
_____

ENRICHMENT ACTIVITY

The attack on Dutch Harbor was big news in Alaska in 1942. Imagine that you are a newspaper journalist putting together a front-page story breaking the news on the attack. What would your headline read? What picture would you use? What would the caption be for that photo?

LEARN MORE

Read more about the attack on Dutch Harbor by visiting
http://www.sitnews.us/0612News/060112/060112_dutch_harbor.html

UNIT 4: CONFLICT IN THE ALEUTIANS

LESSON 11: ENEMY INVADES ATTU

FACTS TO KNOW

Kiska – Island in the Aleutian Chain that Japanese soldiers occupied in June 1942

Charles Foster Jones – 60-year-old radio technician who operated a government radio and weather-reporting station who was captured and killed by Japanese soldiers during the attack on Attu

Etta Jones – Bureau of Indian Affairs teacher who was captured by Japanese soldiers during the attack on Attu and sent to a concentration camp in Japan

COMPREHENSION QUESTIONS

1) What happened two days after the attack on Dutch Harbor on June 6, 1942?
On June 6, 1942, two days after the attack on Dutch Harbor, a Japanese special landing party and 500 troops came ashore at Kiska around 10:30 p.m. They captured a small American naval weather detachment of 10 men, along with a dog. One member of the detachment escaped, but surrendered after 50 days – thin, starving and cold. The enemy then invaded Attu at 3 a.m. on June 7. (Page 130)

2) Explain why the terrain and weather was challenging for both Japanese and American military forces during World War II?
There are approximately 120 volcanic islands comprising the Aleutian Chain. The islands are rocky, barren and covered with spongy tundra or swampy muskeg. Attu usually has a cold, damp fog accompanied by snow or icy rain. Average rainfall measures between 40-50 inches a year. And squalls, called "williwaws," often sweep down the mountains. Winds can reach velocities of more than 100 miles an hour in minutes. (Page 129)

3) What did the Japanese soldiers do to the Aleut people and Etta and Charles Jones?
Most sources agree that Charles Foster Jones was taken by the enemy and never seen again. The villagers were all rounded up and herded to the schoolhouse. The Japanese kept the Aleut fishermen busy for three days supplying the troops with food. Then the villagers were told to grab some food and personal items for themselves, because they were leaving the island. Etta Jones, 62, and the village's 40-plus Aleuts were transported in the hold of a freighter to Hokkaido, Japan, for internment. (Page 131)

4) What were the Aleuts' living conditions like in Japan?
"The Aleuts had no freedom, [and were] held in the same building for the entire war, except the ones who worked in a clay pit near by. The buildings were heated by coal stoves in winter. Hot baths were available whenever the Aleuts wanted them. They slept on the floor on the Japanese standard mats 'Tatami' and they had plenty of blankets." (Page 132)

5) How did half of the Alaska Native prisoners die? What did the Japanese soldiers do with the remaining prisoners?
Tuberculosis later spread widely among the Attuans, despite monthly visits to their camp by a doctor who gave routine examinations and inoculations. Many died. Shortage of fresh food and protein caused starvation and malnutrition. When World War II ended, the surviving 21 Aleuts and one newborn returned to Alaska. Some settled in Akutan, none returned to Attu. (Page 132)

DISCUSSION QUESTION

(Discuss this question with your teacher or write your answer in essay form below. Use additional paper if necessary.)

Why did Japan attack Attu and Kiska?

LEARN MORE

Look for this article at your local library:
"The Aleutians," Alaska Geographic Society, Vol. 7, No. 3, 1980.

MAP ACTIVITY

Locate the follow places from your reading on the map below:

1) Mainland Alaska   2) Russia   3) Japan   4) Bering Sea

5) Unalaska   6) Dutch Harbor   7) Attu   8) Kiska

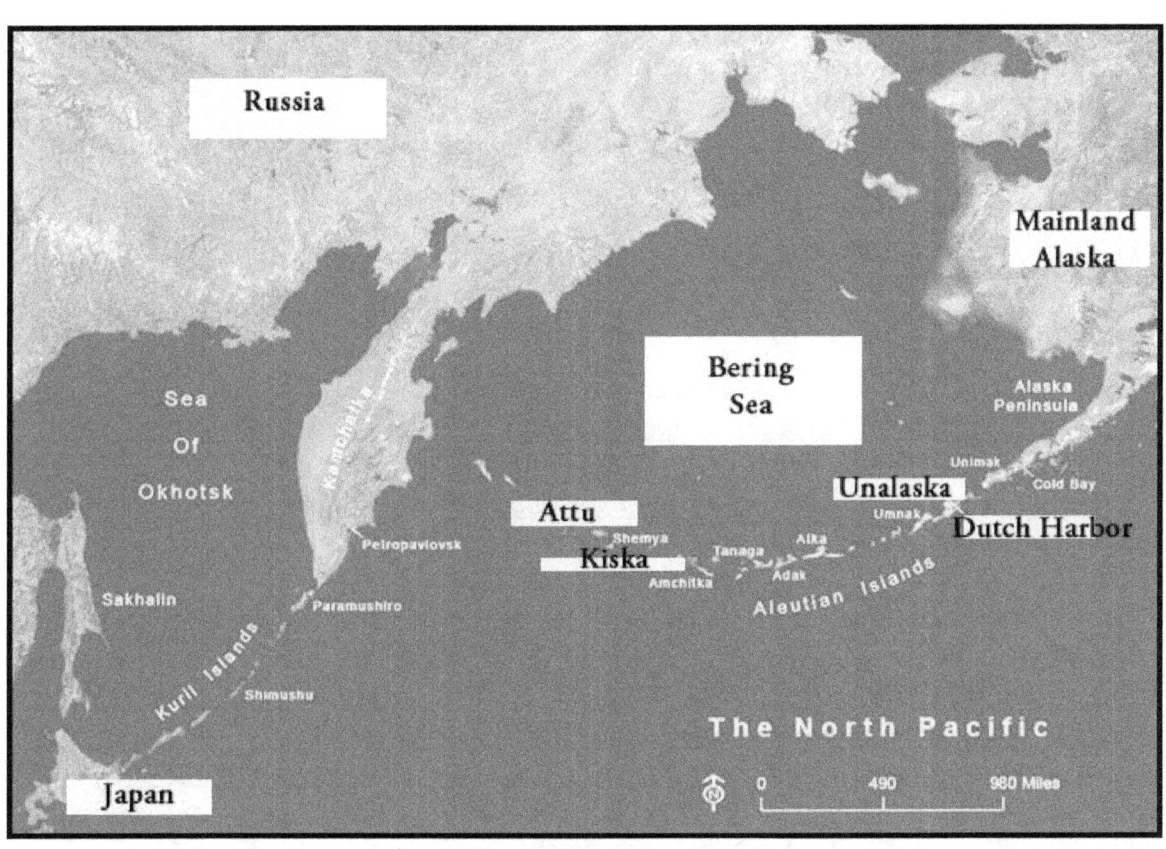

UNIT 4: CONFLICT IN THE ALEUTIANS

LESSON 12: JAPANESE AMERICANS INTERRED

FACTS TO KNOW

Internment – Forced relocation or imprisonment of people who are often seen as a threat

Executive order – Policy signed by the U.S. President that directs the federal government to do something

Minidoka Relocation Center – One of 10 internment camps for Japanese Americans in the U.S.

COMPREHENSION QUESTIONS

1) What was the purpose of Executive Order 9066 signed by U.S. President Franklin D. Roosevelt?
Wartime hysteria and fear of sabotage and espionage ran rampant across the country. President Franklin D. Roosevelt signed Executive Order 9066 in February 1942. It ordered the removal of more than 112,000 Japanese Americans from the West Coast. Those with Japanese ancestry were taken from their homes, businesses and schools and put in internment camps. (Page 135)

2) Describe the conditions at Minidoka Relocation Center. What was the detainees reaction when they arrived?
It was built on a dry, desolate plain. When the detainees arrived at the camp in August 1942, they found it still under construction with no running water or sewer system. "The vast expanse of nothing but sagebrush and dust, a landscape so alien to our eyes, and a desolate, woebegone feeling of being so far removed from home and fireside bogged us down mentally, as well as physically," one evacuee wrote to friends. (Page 136)

3) Why did many people become sick at the internment camp?
There were shortages of food and medicine in the camps, which meant many sick people were left untreated. Some died. At least five other internees were shot and killed because of illness or because they tried to escape, according to government records. (Page 137)

4) How many detainees were American citizens? How long were they detained?
About 60 percent of those interred at Minidoka were U.S.-born American citizens. The remainder, born in Japan, had not yet become naturalized citizens. They were detained for almost two years. (Page 137)

5) What did President Roosevelt's Secretary of the Interior later say about the internment camps?

"As a member of President Roosevelt's administration, I saw the United States Army give way to mass hysteria over the Japanese ... it lost its self-control, and egged on by public clamor, some of it from greedy Americans ... it began to round up indiscriminately the Japanese who had been born in Japan, as well as those born here," he said. "Crowded into cars like cattle, these helpless people were hurried away to hastily constructed and thoroughly inadequate concentration camps, with soldiers with nervous muskets on guard, in the Great American desert." (Pages 138-139)

DISCUSSION QUESTION

(Discuss this question with your teacher or write your answer in essay form below. Use additional paper if necessary.)

How many people were convicted of spying for Japan during the war and where were they from?

_____
_____
_____
_____
_____
_____
_____
_____
_____
_____
_____
_____
_____

ENRICHMENT ACTIVITY

Visit the link below and read 2-3 personal accounts of individuals that were placed in internment camps. Write a short summary of what you learned about what life was like for those that were forced to live in these camps.

https://www.afsc.org/document/afsc-oral-history-project-japanese-american-internment (look for the PDF link at the bottom of the page)

LEARN MORE

Read more about the Japanese internment camps by visiting http://www.pbs.org/childofcamp/history/timeline.html

UNIT 4: CONFLICT IN THE ALEUTIANS

LESSON 13: ALEUTS BECOME REFUGEES

FACTS TO KNOW

Aleuts – Native Alaskans from the Aleutian Islands who also call themselves Unangan
Pribilof Islands – A group of volcanic islands off the coast of mainland Alaska that formerly were called Northern Fur Seal Islands

COMPREHENSION QUESTIONS

1) After the Japanese bombed *Unalaska,* occupied *Kiska* and invaded *Attu* in June 1942, the U.S. military ordered a hasty *evacuation* of more than 800 *Alaska Natives* living in the Aleutian and *Pribilof* islands.

2) Who did the sailors find when they came ashore at Atka? Why were they the only people there?
They only found Office of Indian Affairs schoolteacher Ruby Magee and her husband, Ralph. The couple had urged the villagers to hide after listening to 18 hours of bombing raids on Kiska and sighting a Japanese scout plane. (Page 141)

3) How did Daniel C.R. Benson describe the orders that the sailors were given?
"I was first instructed to prepare the village for destruction that night by placing a pail of gasoline in each house and building, and a charge of dynamite for each other installation such as storage tanks, light plants, trucks, radio transmitters, receivers, antenna masts, etc. The packing of everybody was to be very simple – absolutely nothing but one suitcase per person and a roll of blankets." (Page 142)

4) Where were the Aleuts taken?
They decided to drop entire villages at different locations in Southeast Alaska. Atkans were assigned an abandoned cannery on Killisnoo Island and the Pribilof people were to settle deserted facilities nearby. All 480 Pribilof residents debarked in Funter Bay. Evacuees from St. Paul were housed in an abandoned fish cannery and the community of St. George in an abandoned gold mining camp a few miles away. (Page 144)

5) Describe some of the conditions at the duration villages.
Families lived in poorly insulated rooms, partitioned by blankets. Rats and mice often scurried across the bare floors. One toilet, which sat over the beach just above the low tide mark, served 90 percent of the evacuees. All the human waste washed directly into

the bay, contaminating the water. Food was scarce. And until that fall, people slept in relays. There were no mops or brooms to clean up. There was no place to shower or wash clothing. (Pages 144-145)

6) Why did the Aleut people hate the area that the miltary brought them to be safe?
For the most part, the people hated the densely forested land of Southeast filled with stands of 150-foot spruce, cedar and hemlock. They were used to the windswept, treeless plains and beaches of the Aleutians where vegetation grew no taller than waist high. (Page 153)

DISCUSSION QUESTION

(Discuss this question with your teacher or write your answer in essay form below. Use additional paper if necessary.)

In what major industry were the Aleuts forced to work in the Pribilof Islands?

_____
_____
_____
_____
_____
_____
_____
_____
_____
_____
_____
_____
_____
_____
_____
_____
_____
_____
_____

ENRICHMENT ACTIVITY

What similarities and differences do you see between the internment of Japanese Americans and the Aleuts during World War II? Write at least two paragraphs to compare and contrast these two events in history.

LEARN MORE

The Treatment of the Aleuts: A World War II Tragedy. Anchorage, Alaska: The Aleutian/ Pribilof Islands Association

UNIT 4: CONFLICT IN THE ALEUTIANS

LESSON 14: ENEMY OUSTED FROM ALEUTIANS

FACTS TO KNOW

Attu – 40-mile island on the westernmost tip of the Aleutians where the U.S. military made its first-ever amphibious landing

Massacre Bay – One of the landing points where U.S. troops attacked Japanese soldiers

COMPREHENSION QUESTIONS

1) Why did the U.S. military send 15,000 troops to Attu in May 1943?
About 15,000 troops began assembling at the beginning of May, four segments getting ready for the assault on the 40-mile island of Attu. One would be a reserve regiment, while the other three segments would hit Red Beach, Holtz Bay and Massacre Bay. (Page 166)

2) What happened when the troops got to Massacre Bay?
The Japanese lay in lines, holed in along the brow of the pass and along the ridges. They watched the Americans land, and soon heavy, accurate machine-gun fire came thundering down. Next day, the huge guns of the American battleship Nevada returned the fire, chewing great hunks out of the mountain. (Pages 166-167)

3) How long was the battle expected to last? How long did it last? How many American soldiers lost their lives?
The battle was expected to last a few days. It lasted for weeks. Before the battle was over, there would be 549 American and 2,351 Japanese dead. (Page 169)

4) What did many Japanese soldiers do to prevent being captured by U.S. soldiers?
When their attack failed, 500 men committed mass suicide by pulling the pins of their grenades and holding them against their chests and heads. When cornered, most chose death rather than capture. Only 28 prisoners were taken at Attu. (Page 172)

5) What happened during the invasion of Kiska in 1943?
There was no opposition to the 32,000 U.S. and Canadian forces because no Japanese troops were left on the island. Under cover of fog, the Japanese fleet had secretly removed its 5,000 soldiers from Kiska by I-class submarines and surface vessels prior to the Allied attack. Allied casualties during the invasion still numbered close to 200, however, as the enemy had set booby traps prior to leaving Kiska. A mine in the harbor sunk a destroyer,

killing 72 men. Another 17 Americans and four Canadians were killed from either booby traps or friendly fire, and 50 wounded. Trench foot infected about 130 men. (Page 173)

DISCUSSION QUESTION

(Discuss this question with your teacher or write your answer in essay form below. Use additional paper if necessary.)

Thousands of soldiers lost their lives during World War II. What are some ways that we can remember those that lost their lives during war?

_____
_____
_____
_____
_____
_____
_____
_____
_____
_____
_____
_____
_____
_____
_____

TIME TO REVIEW

Review Chapters 10-14 of your book before moving on the Unit Review. See how many questions you can answer without looking at your book.

UNIT 4: CONFLICT IN THE ALEUTIANS

REVIEW LESSONS 10-14

Write down what you remember about:

Dutch Harbor – *Area on Unalaska Island that was attacked by Japanese troops in 1942*

Japanese Zeros – *Fighter aircraft also known as Mitsubishi A6M or Navy Type 0*

Code breakers – *Military personnel trained to interpret encrypted messages*

Kiska – *Island in the Aleutian Chain that Japanese soldiers occupied in June 1942*

Charles Foster Jones – *60-year-old radio technician who operated a government radio and weather-reporting station and was captured and killed by Japanese soldiers during the attack on Attu*

Etta Jones – *Bureau of Indian Affairs teacher who was captured by Japanese soldiers during the attack on Attu and sent to a concentration camp in Japan*

Internment – *Forced relocation or imprisonment of people who are often seen as a threat*

Executive order – *Policy signed by the U.S. President that directs the federal government to do something*

Minidoka Relocation Center – *One of 10 internment camps for Japanese Americans in the U.S.*

Aleuts – *Native Alaskans from the Aleutian Islands who also call themselves Unangan*

Pribilof Islands – *A group of volcanic islands off the coast of mainland Alaska that formerly were called Northern Fur Seal Islands*

Attu – *40-mile island on the westernmost tip of the Aleutians where the U.S. military made its first-ever amphibious landing*

Massacre Bay – *One of the landing points where U.S. troops attacked Japanese soldiers*

Fill in the blanks:

1) *Japanese* troops invaded the *Aleutian* Islands in June *1942*. During the two-day attack, *33* U.S. soldiers and sailors, as well as 10 civilians, died. But the devastation at *Dutch* Harbor could have been worse. Rear Adm. Kakuji Kakuta had dispatched more than *30 planes* from two small aircraft carriers. Due to *fog, high seas and strong winds*, less than half the planes reached the islands.

2) American *code breakers* learned in mid-March that the *Japanese* planned to bomb, and then *occupy*, the *Aleutians*.

3) On June *6, 1942*, two days after the attack on *Dutch* Harbor, a Japanese special landing party and 500 troops came ashore at *Kiska* around 10:30 p.m.

4) The Japanese kept the *Aleut* fishermen busy for three days supplying the troops with food. Then the villagers were told to grab some *food and personal items* for themselves, because they were *leaving the island*. They were kept in the unpleasant-smelling hold of a ship for the weeklong *voyage*, never seeing daylight until they reached *Japan*.

5) The *Aleutian* Islands are *rocky, barren and covered with spongy tundra* or swampy muskeg. Attu has high *mountainous* terrain, rising 3,000 feet, starting close to its shoreline and stretching into the interior of the island. It usually has a cold, damp *fog* accompanied by *snow or icy rain*.

6) *U.S. President Franklin D. Roosevelt* signed Executive Order 9066 in February 1942. It ordered the *removal* of more than 112,000 Japanese Americans from the West Coast. Those with *Japanese* ancestry were taken from their homes, businesses and schools and put in *internment camps*.

7) U.S. authorities evacuated hundreds of men, women and children from the *Aleutian* and *Pribilof* islands following the Japanese attacks on *Dutch Harbor, Kiska and Attu*. These people were relocated to "*duration villages*" in Southeast Alaska.

8) For most of the camps, *school* for the children and *contact* with the outside world was sparse. The evacuees lacked *warm winter clothes, adequate diets and medicine to combat diseases that ran rampant*.

9) In May _1943_, Americans finally dislodged the enemy from its toehold on the _westernmost_ tip of the _Aleutians_. They did it in a battle that became – in proportion to the number of opposing troops – the second most _costly war in lives lost_ in the Pacific, second only to Iwo Jima.

10) It was a tricky campaign; the _island's terrain_ was almost as hard to conquer as the enemy, and the _fog and mist and eternal raw chill_ took their toll as well as the enemy bullets. By the seventh day of battle, _American troops_ had suffered 1,100 casualties, 500 of them from exposure. Before the battle was over, there would be 549 _American_ and 2,351 _Japanese_ dead.

11) On Aug. 15, 1943, the Allied invasion of _Kiska_ began. But there was no _opposition_ to the 32,000 U.S. and Canadian forces because no _Japanese_ troops were left on the island. Under _cover of fog_, the _Japanese_ fleet had secretly removed its 5,000 soldiers from _Kiska_ by I-class submarines and surface vessels prior to the Allied attack.

Japanese Attack Aleutians
Word Search Puzzle Key
Find the words listed below

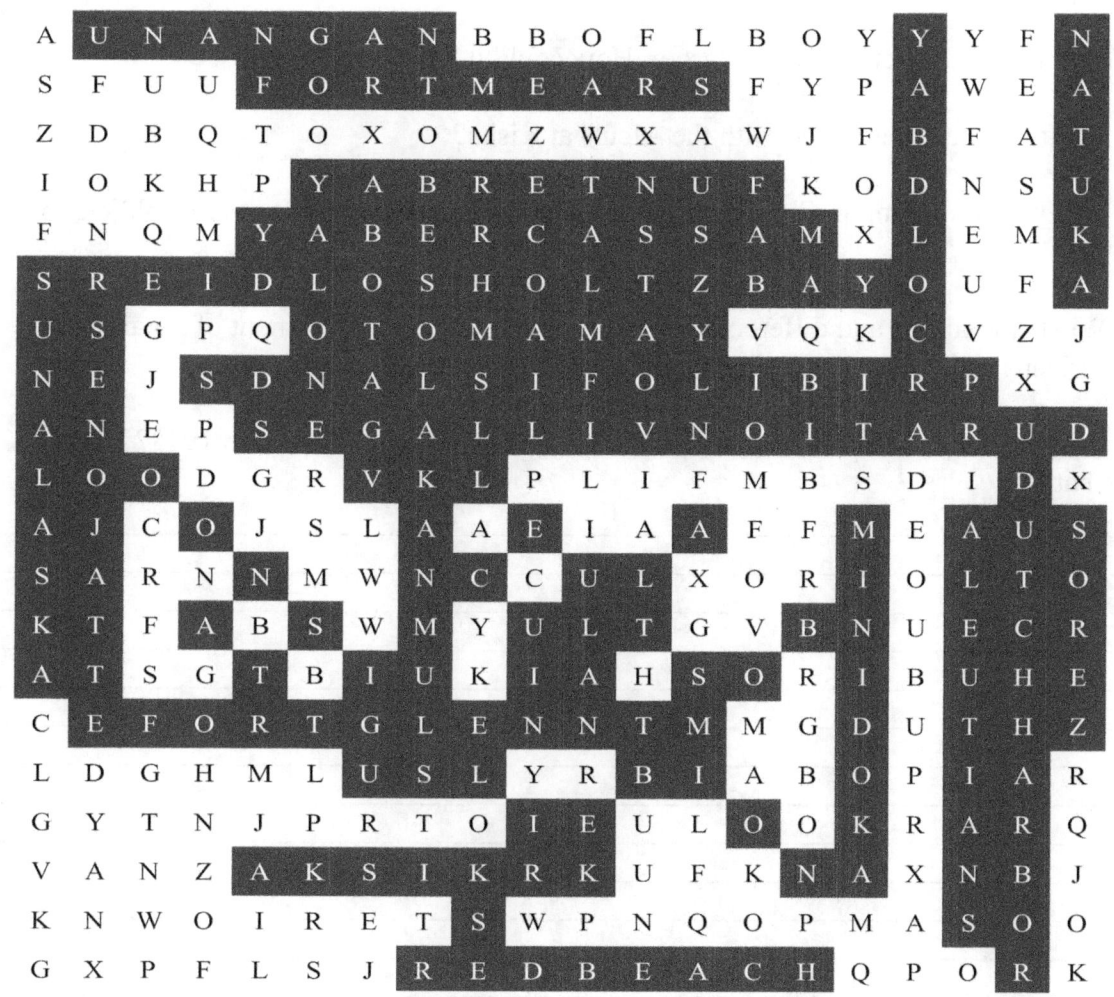

DUTCH HARBOR UNALASKA ATTU FUNTER BAY AKUTAN
KISKA FORT MEARS ZEROS EVACUATION RED BEACH
BOMBERS ALEUTIANS YAMAMOTO MASSACRE BAY ALLIES
FORT GLENN UMNAK COLD BAY UNANGAN
ETTA JONES ALEUTS MINIDOKA HOLTZ BAY
DURATION VILLAGES PRIBILOF ISLANDS KILLISNOO SOLDIERS

UNIT 4: CONFLICT IN THE ALEUTIANS

UNIT TEST

Choose *three* of the following questions to answer in paragraph form. Use as much detail as possible to completely answer the question.

1) Describe the attack at Dutch Harbor. How could it have been worse?

2) What did the Japanese do with the Aleuts at Kiska?

3) Why was the Aleutian Chain a difficult place for both U.S. and Japanese soldiers to battle?

4) What similarities and differences do you see between the internment of Japanese Americans and the Aleuts during World War II?

5) Why did the United States send 15,000 troops to the island of Attu in 1943? Describe the battle.

TEACHER NOTES ABOUT THIS UNIT

TEACHER NOTES ABOUT THIS UNIT

UNIT 5: 1940s POSTWAR NEWS

LESSON 15: 1945: DISCRIMINATION TORPEDOED

FACTS TO KNOW

Segregation – Process of separating people of different races or religions from each other

Alberta Schenck – Civil rights activist for Native rights who was discriminated against in a Nome theater

The 1867 Treaty of Cessions – Declared Alaska Natives were not deemed U.S. citizens because they were "uncivilized"

COMPREHENSION QUESTIONS

1) Describe the segregation that Alaska Natives were subjected to in the 1900s. What other race experienced similar discrimination in the United States?
Just like African-Americans in many of the contiguous United States, Alaska Natives had separate entrances, designated seating areas and different bathrooms than whites in public areas. (Page 176)

2) What event in Nome brought a spotlight on the discrimination against Alaska Natives?
In 1944, the Dreamland movie theater's manager told Alberta Schenck to move to the "Native's only" section of the theater. Her date told her to stay put. The manager then called the chief of police, who arrived shortly thereafter and forcibly removed the young lady from the theater. He shoved her out into the bitter-cold arctic night and tossed her into jail. (Page 177)

3) How did Maj. Marston get involved in this case? What was the result?
Maj. Marston said Alberta and her family came to him seeking advice about legal counsel for a lawsuit. He told Alberta to send her statement of the night's events to Alaska Territorial Governor Ernest Gruening at Juneau. The governor wired back, "A mistake has been made. It won't happen again." (Page 179)

4) Who were the Alaska Native Brotherhood and Sisterhood? What injustices did they fight? *The Alaska Native Brotherhood, organized by 12 Tlingit Natives from Southeast Alaska in 1912, began working toward changing perceptions about Alaska's Native people. Alaska Native Sisterhood organized a few years later. Both groups worked tirelessly to advocate for the civil rights of Alaska Natives, and eventually the groups became powerful political forces in the territory. (Pages 180-181)*

5) Why do Alaskan's celebrate Elizabeth Peratrovich Day?
As Grand Camp President of the Alaska Native Sisterhood, Elizabeth Peratrovich provided the crucial testimony that cultivated passage of the Anti-Discrimination Bill on Feb. 16, 1945, with a vote of 11-5. (Pages 182-184)

DISCUSSION QUESTION

(Discuss this question with your teacher or write your answer in essay form below. Use additional paper if necessary.)

How do you think segregation affects a society?

_____
_____
_____
_____
_____
_____
_____
_____
_____
_____
_____
_____
_____
_____
_____
_____
_____

ENRICHMENT ACTIVITY

Choose one article from the link below to read more about segregation in Alaska. Take notes about what you are reading, and prepare a 2-3-minute oral report about what you read.

LEARN MORE

Read more about segregation in Alaska by visiting
http://www.alaskool.org/projects/JimCrow/Jimcrow.htm

UNIT 5: 1940s POSTWAR NEWS

LESSON 16: 1947: REEVE AIRWAYS TAKES FLIGHT

FACTS TO KNOW

Robert "Bob" Campbell Reeve – Bush pilot who started Reeve Airways
Reeve Aleutian Airways – Airline that served the Aleutian Chain

COMPREHENSION QUESTIONS

1) Why was Robert Reeve's nickname "Glacier Pilot"?
His 2,000-some glacier landings earned him the nickname "Glacier Pilot." (Page 188)

2) How did Robert Reeve fall in love with flying? How did he get to Alaska?
While stationed at Camp Custer in Michigan, Reeve paid $5 to ride in an airplane for five minutes. That five minutes changed his life. Aviation entered his blood. While in South America, he heard tales about Alaska that enticed him north. Following a short visit in the states, and a bout with polio that bothered one leg for years, he stowed away on a steamer and arrived in Anchorage. (Pages 188-189)

3) What event in 1937 caused him to stop glacier landings?
While ferrying the Washburn Expedition of 1937 to Mount Lucania in Canada, Reeve landed on a glacier at an altitude of 8,750 feet – more than 1,800 feet higher than any other plane had landed with passengers and freight, according to Stan Cohen, author of "Flying Beats Work: The Story of Reeve Aleutian Airways." Due to an unusually warm winter, much snow had melted, and the plane sunk belly-deep in the slush. Reeve waited a week for the weather to cool so he could take off. (Page 189)

4) How did Robert Reeve start Reeve Aleutian Airways?
As Reeve learned about the Aleutian weather, islands and coastlines, he formed a plan to serve the 1,783-mile Aleutian route with scheduled air service. Following the end of World War II, Reeve bought a surplus DC-3 C-47 from the U.S. Air Force and converted it for civilian use. His fledgling business took off following a steamship strike. He and his two pilots made 26 roundtrip flights between either Anchorage or Fairbanks and Seattle in 53 days. The bush pilot's airline grew during the 1950s and 1960s as it acquired leases to many old military airfields down the Aleutian Chain. (Pages 191-192)

DISCUSSION QUESTION

(Discuss this question with your teacher or write your answer in essay form below. Use additional paper if necessary.)

What can we learn from Robert Reeve's story of going from a poor young stowaway, to a distinguished bush pilot and the owner of an airline?

_____
_____
_____
_____
_____
_____
_____
_____
_____
_____
_____
_____
_____
_____
_____
_____
_____
_____

ENRICHMENT ACTIVITY

Read more about Robert Reeve on the National Aviation Hall of Fame Website using the link below. See if you can find one other inductee on the Website that you read about in your textbook: http://www.nationalaviation.org/our-enshrinees/reeve-robert/

LEARN MORE

Look for this book at your local library:
Glacier Pilot. Beth Day. Garden City, New Jersey: 1974.

UNIT 5: 1940s POSTWAR NEWS

LESSON 17: 1948: MURDERER NOMINATED KING

FACTS TO KNOW

Anchorage Fur Rendezvous – Annual winter festival in Anchorage
Jacob Marunenko – Also known as "Jack Marchin" or "Russian Jack"

COMPREHENSION QUESTIONS

1) What are some of the events that occurred in Anchorage during the 1920s and 1930s?
The Alaska Railroad was finished in 1923. During the 1920s and 1930s several of Anchorage's future prominent citizens moved to town. Another Russian immigrant named Z.J. "Zack" Loussac relocated from Iditarod and started a drug store that made him wealthy beyond his dreams; John and Marie Bagoy built a greenhouse that supplied the community with fresh-cut flowers and vegetables; and a young reporter named Robert Atwood arrived. (Pages 195-196)

2) Where was Jacob Marunenko from? How did he earn a living in Alaska?
Marunenko had left a wife and two small children in the Ukrainian village of Parevka in the early 1900s when he headed to the Last Frontier. earning a living doing carpentry and hauling wood. He also earned money making moonshine in an illegal still on his homestead property. (Pages 194-196)

3) Summarize his account of events on March 22, 1937?
"Russian Jack" admitted firing the shot that sent a bullet through Hamilton's brain and killed him instantly. But he testified that he had no intention of killing the man. He claimed that taxi driver Milton Hamilton attacked him and he shot off a warning shot to scare him which killed the man. (Pages 196-199)

4) What was the result of the case against him for this incident?
The jury found Marchin not guilty of first-degree murder, but guilty of manslaughter and recommended leniency. Judge Simon Hellenthal sentenced Marchin to 2-1/2 years in the federal penitentiary at McNeil Island, Wash. (Page 199)

5) What honor did "Russian Jack" receive during the Anchorage Fur Rendezvous?
Marchin was nominated for Mardi Gras King. He lost the election to Kurly Braga, but he was named prince of the events. His popularity indicates that most of the community felt Marchin had paid his debt to society and welcomed him back. (Page 200)

DISCUSSION QUESTION

(Discuss this question with your teacher or write your answer in essay form below. Use additional paper if necessary.)

Can you name another person in history whose past crimes did not stop them from being honored later in life for the good things that they did?

ENRICHMENT ACTIVITY

Creatively narrate the story of Russian Jack by either writing a poem, drawing a picture, making a storyboard, etc. Share your narration with the class.

LEARN MORE

Read more about Russian Jack by visiting
http://www.alaskahistory.org/biographies/marunenko-jacob-russian-jack/

UNIT 5: 1940s POSTWAR NEWS

LESSON 18: 1948: ALASKA AIRLINES MAKES HISTORY

FACTS TO KNOW

Alaska Airlines – Famous airline that began as McGee Airlines in 1932
Linious "Mac" McGee – Fur trader who started Alaska Airlines
Berlin Airlift – Airlines delivered much needed supplies to Berlin after the Soviet Union blocked all rail and road access to the German city

COMPREHENSION QUESTIONS

1) Describe how Linious McGee and Harvey Barnhill started the airline.
Fur trader Linious "Mac" McGee, along with reputedly hard-drinking bush pilot Harvey "Barney" Barnhill, bought a three-seat Stinson in 1931 for $5,000 in San Francisco. The next year he advertised in the Anchorage Daily Times that McGee Airways also offered charter service between Anchorage and Bristol Bay. "Fly an Hour or Walk a Week," the ad stated. (Pages 202-203)

2) What concept did Linious McGee pioneer as he purchased more airplanes for the airline?
He pioneered the concept of building a fleet of identical airplanes so the parts would be interchangeable. (Page 203)

3) When did the airline become Alaska Airlines?
The airline became Alaska Airlines in 1944. When the corporation sold the airlines to wealthy New York wheeler-dealer R.W. Marshall in 1942, the new owner changed the name again and it became Alaska Star Airlines. Two years later, he dropped the middle name. (Page 205)

4) How did Alaska Airlines help the city of Berlin?
Manager James Wooten landed the company a lucrative deal during the Berlin Airlift to ferry tons of lifesaving supplies into Berlin after the Soviet Union blocked all rail and road access to the German city. (Pages 205-206)

5) What was Operation Magic Carpet? How did Alaska Airlines get involved?

The government of Israel, established in 1947 when the United Nations passed a resolution to partition Palestine, mounted airlift operations in 1949 to bring Jewish people to the new country after the Imam of Yemen agreed to let 45,000 Jews leave his country. Operating on a charter basis, Alaska Airlines joined other carriers and shuttled Jews from Aden, the capital of Yemen, to their new homeland. (Pages 207-208)

DISCUSSION QUESTION

(Discuss this question with your teacher or write your answer in essay form below. Use additional paper if necessary.)

How did involvement in the Berlin Airlift and Operation Magic Carpet benefit Alaska Airlines (other than monetarily)?

_____
_____
_____
_____
_____
_____
_____
_____
_____
_____
_____
_____
_____
_____
_____
_____
_____
_____

ENRICHMENT ACTIVITY

Using the information that you read in Chapter 18, create a timeline of events for Alaska Airlines beginning at the founding of McGee Airlines.

LEARN MORE

Read more about Alaska Airlines involvement with Operation Magic Carpet by reading https://www.alaskaair.com/content/about-us/history/magic-carpet.aspx

UNIT 5: 1940s POSTWAR NEWS

LESSON 19: IN OTHER NEWS ...

COMPREHENSION QUESTIONS

Write one or two sentences about each of the following events:

1) **1940: Sydney Laurence Dies** *Known for his dramatic landscape paintings, Laurence was one of the first professionally trained artists to live in the territory. His works, which often featured Mt. McKinley, hang in the Musee du Louvre in Paris, the National Art Gallery in Washington, D.C., and many other locations around the world. He died on September 12, 1940.* (Pages 212-213)

2) **1943: Venetie Reservation** *Created In 1943, U.S. Secretary of the Interior Harold L. Ickes created the Venetie Reservation. Through combined efforts of the remaining residents of Venetie, Arctic Village, Christian Village and Robert's Fish Camp, the Venetie Indian Reservation was established to protect the land for subsistence use.* (Pages 214-215)

3) **1944: Alaska-Juneau Gold Mine Shuts Down** *Although the federal War Production Board ordered the closure of all nonessential mines to free up men for the World War II effort in 1942, it allowed the Alaska-Juneau Gold Mine to continue its operation. But the operating costs proved too high to continue mining at rock-bottom prices, so the massive mine closed in 1944.* (Page 216)

4) **1945: Floating Clinics Take to Alaska Waters** *The ships traveled between rural coastal communities each spring and/or fall. The doctors radioed ahead to let villagers know when they expected to be in port. The local people then would board for checkups and medical care, including teeth-pulling, shots and X-rays.* (Page 218)

5) **1947: Kake Becomes First Incorporated School District** *Kake, located 95 air miles southwest of Juneau in Southeast Alaska, became Alaska's first independently incorporated school for Native children in 1947.* (Page 219)

6) **1947: Southeast Natives File Land Claims Suit** *In 1947, Tlingit and Haida people filed the first land claims suit in the U.S. court of claims. Southeast Alaska Natives wanted to get back their land and ensure subsistence use for future generations.* (Page 220)

TIME TO REVIEW

Review Chapters 15-19 of your book before moving on the Unit Review. See how many questions you can answer without looking at your book.

UNIT 5: 1940s POSTWAR NEWS

REVIEW LESSONS 15-19

Write down what you remember about:

Segregation – *Process of separating people of different races or religions from each other*

Alberta Schenck – *Civil rights activist for Native rights who was discriminated against in a Nome theater*

The 1867 Treaty of Cessions – *Declared Alaska Natives were not deemed U.S. citizens because they were "uncivilized"*

Robert "Bob" Campbell Reeve – *Bush pilot who started Reeve Airways*

Reeve Aleutian Airways – *Airline that served the Aleutian Chain*

Anchorage Fur Rendezvous – *Annual winter festival in Anchorage*

Jacob Marunenko – *Also known as "Jack Marchin" or "Russian Jack"*

Alaska Airlines – *Famous airline that began as McGee Airlines in 1932*

Linious "Mac" McGee – *Fur trader who started Alaska Airlines*

Berlin Airlift – *Airlines delivered much needed supplies to Berlin after the Soviet Union blocked all rail and road access to the German city*

Fill in the blanks:

1) Even though Alaska's *Native people* served with distinction guarding Alaska's borders, *segregation* thrived throughout the territory. Just like *African-Americans* in many of the contiguous United States, *Alaska Natives* had separate *entrances, designated seating areas and different bathrooms* than whites in public areas.

2) *Alberta Schenck* had bucked the long-held status quo and dared to sit in the *"white only"* section of the theater. She wrote about the injustices directed toward *Alaska's Natives* in an essay for her high school history class. It was published in The *Nome* Nugget newspaper.

3) *Elizabeth Peratrovich*, an Alaska Native, was instrumental in the passage of the Anti-*Discrimination* Act in *1945*. Then the Molly Hootch case of 1976 ended more *discrimination* by allowing schools to be built in *Native* communities.

4) One of Alaska's most respected *bush pilots* launched his own *airline* with a 21-passenger Douglas DC-3 C-47 Skytrain Dakota purchased from the U.S. Air Force in March 1947. *Robert "Bob" Cambell Reeve* birthed *Reeve Aleutian Airways Inc.* to serve the people of the Aleutian Chain.

5) *Robert Reeve* pioneered new flight routes to get to hard-to-reach *mines*, developed a method for landing on mud flats with skis and set down on many *glaciers and icefields*. His 2,000-some *glacier* landings earned him the nickname *"Glacier Pilot."*

6) In 1948, one of Anchorage's most colorful characters, *Jacob Marunenko*, was nominated for *Mardi Gras King* during the Anchorage *Fur Rendezvous*. Known as *Russian Jack*, this homesteader also was a *murderer*.

7) In his account of events during his trial, *Jacob Marunenko* explained that he shot *Milton Hamilton* while being choked. "Russian Jack" admitted firing the shot that killed *Hamilton* instantly. But he testified that *he had no intention* of killing the man.

8) Alaska Airlines flew into the history books when, in 1948, it participated in the *Berlin Airlift.* Manager *James Wooten's* efforts landed the company a lucrative deal during the *Berlin Airlift* to ferry tons of *lifesaving supplies* into *Berlin* after the Soviet Union blocked all rail and road access to the German city.

9) *Alaska Airlines* carried up to 150 people per trip during Operation *Magic Carpet*. The government of *Israel*, established in 1947 when the United Nations passed a resolution to partition *Palestine*, mounted airlift operations in 1949 to bring *Jewish* people to the new country after the Imam of Yemen agreed to let 45,000 *Jews* leave his country.

1940s People of Influence
Word Scramble Puzzle Key
Unscramble the words below

1.	alarbet cnecshk	alberta schenck	Bucked the status quo and sat in the "white only" section of Nome movie theater
2.	wmiilal ulpa	william paul	First Alaska Native to serve in the Alaska Territorial Legislature
3.	thibeaezl vrpcoihrate	elizabeth peratrovich	Alaska Native woman who was instrumental in passage of Anti-Discrimination Bill in 1945
4.	brrote veree	robert reeve	Started an airline to serve the Aleutian Chain and was known as the Glacier Pilot
5.	rnisuas jkac	russian jack	Anchorage character who murdered a man and still became the Mardi Gras King of the Anchorage Fur Rendezvous
6.	uionlis cgeme	linious mcgee	Acknowledged founder of Alaska Airlines
7.	terorb sllie	robert ellis	Started an airlines in Ketchikan in 1936
8.	ikkr rtipcrikak	kirk kirpatrick	Began Cordova Airlines in 1934
9.	dnyeys eacrnleu	sydney laurence	Legendary Alaska artist known for dramatic landscape paintings
10.	restne ggiernnu	ernest gruening	Territorial governor who signed Anti-Discrimination Bill into law in 1945

UNIT 5: 1940s POSTWAR NEWS

UNIT TEST

Choose *two* of the following questions to answer in paragraph form. Use as much detail as possible to completely answer the question.

1) Describe segregation and discrimination that Alaska Natives experienced in the 1900s.

2) How did Robert Reeve start Reeve Airways? What else was he famous for?

3) Who was Russian Jack? Describe the events that led to his conviction in 1937.

4) What are some ways that Alaska Airlines made history? Explain at least one of these events in detail.

5) Describe at least two other important events in Alaska history that you read about in this unit and have not written about in this test.

TEACHER NOTES ABOUT THIS UNIT

UNIT 6: COLD WAR ERA

LESSON 20: 'RED SCARE' BRINGS BOOM

FACTS TO KNOW

Union of Soviet Socialist Republics –Rival of the United States with nuclear power
Distant Early Warning System – Radar network designed to warn Alaska of nuclear attack

COMPREHENSION QUESTIONS

1) What was the "red scare"?
"Red Scare" gripped the nation following World War II. The Union of Soviet Socialist Republics, an ally during the war, became an international rival armed with nuclear power after it exploded its first atomic bomb and built an intercontinental bomber in late 1949. (Page 222)

2) Why did Alaska become the "eyes" of the nation in the 1940s?
Alaska, offering the shortest route for a Soviet attack on America, became the "eyes" of the nation. Congress quickly appropriated money to build up Alaska Air Command facilities, which included an Aircraft Control and Warning system in the Last Frontier. (Pages 222-223)

3) How did military spending in the 1950s connect Alaska's communities?
Soon Alaska's sparse communities became connected in a way that never could have happened without military money. Radio and telephone support systems for the Distant Early Warning System, called the DEW line, popped up on the tundra, as Alaska Integrated Communications Enterprise linked communications between the DEW line and aircraft warning networks. They also brought television, radio and telephone communications. (Pages 226-227)

4) How did the Alaska Railroad benefit from military spending?
An old roundhouse in Fairbanks was transformed into a $7.5 million terminal; Anchorage received a diesel-mechanical building, power plant and employee housing; steel bridges replaced wooden ones along the route, and hundreds of miles of 115-pound rails were laid where 70-pound ones had worn out between Anchorage and Fairbanks and Anchorage and Seward. (Page 228)

5) How did the Alaska road system benefit from military spending?
Between 1945 and 1952, the Glenn Highway was improved and blacktopped, the Richardson Highway was rebuilt and hard-surfaced, the road between Seward and Anchorage was built, the Alaska-Canada Highway opened to civilian traffic and the Sterling Highway connected Homer to the road system. (Page 228)

DISCUSSION QUESTION

(Discuss this question with your teacher or write your answer in essay form below. Use additional paper if necessary.)

How did increased military presence in the 1950s affect Alaska's economy?

_____
_____
_____
_____
_____
_____
_____
_____
_____
_____
_____
_____
_____
_____
_____
_____
_____
_____

ENRICHMENT ACTIVITY

Imagine that you are living in Alaska in the 1950s and experiencing all the changes to your community (improved communication, transportation, etc.). Write a short story or diary entry about your experience.

LEARN MORE

The Opening of Alaska. William L. "Billy" Mitchell. Edited by Lyman L. Woodman. Anchorage: Cook Inlet Historical Society, 1982.

UNIT 6: COLD WAR ERA

LESSON 21: ANCHORAGE: JEWEL ON THE TUNDRA

FACTS TO KNOW

    Anchorage Light and Power Co. –Anchorage power company had to increase production for the fast-increasing population

    Tundra – A vast, flat, treeless region in which the subsoil is permanently frozen

COMPREHENSION QUESTIONS

1) Why did people pour into Anchorage in the 1950s?
Servicemen and women who had been stationed in Alaska chose to remain after World War II, and additional military projects during the Cold War era brought thousands more construction workers north. (Page 230)

2) What problems did the large increase in population cause?
Anchorage found itself playing catch-up to a demand for services and goods as frame houses sprang up all over the area. Reliable power for the growing populace soon became a major problem. Blackouts became frequent, prices were high and many homes had no electricity at all. (Page 231)

3) How did the people of Anchorage trick U.S. Postmaster General James A. Farley into recommending the building of a Federal Building?
It all began when the townspeople learned that U.S. Postmaster General James A. Farley was slated to visit Anchorage in 1936. To highlight the woefully inadequate post office, built in 1915, some local leaders lugged all the good furniture out of the building and replaced it with broken tables, cracked chairs and other pieces that had seen better days. And signs announcing "Unsafe," "Condemned," "Dangerous" and "Watch Out for Falling Debris" were nailed up for good measure. The plan worked. (Page 236)

4) According to Clifford Cernick, how were the average statesider's conception of Anchorage challenged with all of the changes to the city?
"The average statesider's conception of life in the 'ice-locked land of glaciers, totem poles and Eskimos' is shattered forever when he notes the city's modern buildings, its three radio stations, three theaters, two newspapers and well-stocked shops." (Page 240)

5) Why was Anchorage the first city outside of the contiguous 48 states to be named an "All-America City"?

The National Municipal League and Look magazine named Anchorage an "All-America City" in 1956 for "successfully tackling a skyrocketing population that threatened to swamp city facilities and pushing for needed civic improvements." It was the first time that any city outside of the contiguous 48 states had been so honored. (Page 244)

DISCUSSION QUESTION

(Discuss this question with your teacher or write your answer in essay form below. Use additional paper if necessary.)

What were the typical prices for a meal in Anchorage in 1950? How does this compare to prices today?

___

ENRICHMENT ACTIVITY

Imagine that you are a journalist for a national newspaper. Write a short newspaper story covering Anchorage being named All-America City in 1956. Include several reasons for why the city received this honor.

LEARN MORE

Anchorage: All American City. Evangeline Atwood. Binfords and Mort. 1957

UNIT 6: COLD WAR ERA

LESSON 22: OTHER ALASKA TOWNS GROW

COMPREHENSION QUESTIONS

Write one to two sentences about how each city benefited from defense spending during the 1950s.

1) **Fairbanks** *Fairbanks saw a post-war boom through the construction of Eielson Air Force Base and the enlargement of Ladd Air Force Base. Those projects brought more military personnel to Alaska's largest Interior city, which meant work for local residents and sales for city merchants. (Page 247)*

2) **Nome** *As the chief distributing center for Northwestern Alaska, military activity spurred construction of a new hospital, seawall and a few new hotels. (Page 248)*

3) **Seward** *As the ocean terminal for the Alaska Railroad, Seward's population grew during and after World War II. The Seward Highway, completed in 1951, finally connected Seward to Anchorage and Alaska's growing road system. (Page 249)*

4) **Valdez** *The building and improvements made to the Richardson Highway during the postwar years brought new life to the fishing community. (Page 250)*

5) **Kodiak** *Kodiak, home of a chief naval base in Alaska, received millions in government spending between 1950 and 1960 for a satellite tracking system. Military personnel comprised most of the 8,000 people in the district – the town itself only had about 2,000 residents. (Page 250)*

6) **Sitka** *One of the oldest towns in Alaska, Sitka reaped a renewal during the war and postwar years. The U.S. military built a naval base on Japonski Island, and the federal government spent millions on hospitals, schools and other institutions in the coastal town of 3,000. (Page 252)*

7) **Skagway** *As the terminus for the White Pass & Yukon Railway, its deserted streets filled with nearly 3,000 military men who guarded the coast and built the Alaska-Canada Highway. (Page 253)*

MAP ACTIVITY

Locate each of the cities listed on Page 80 on the map below:

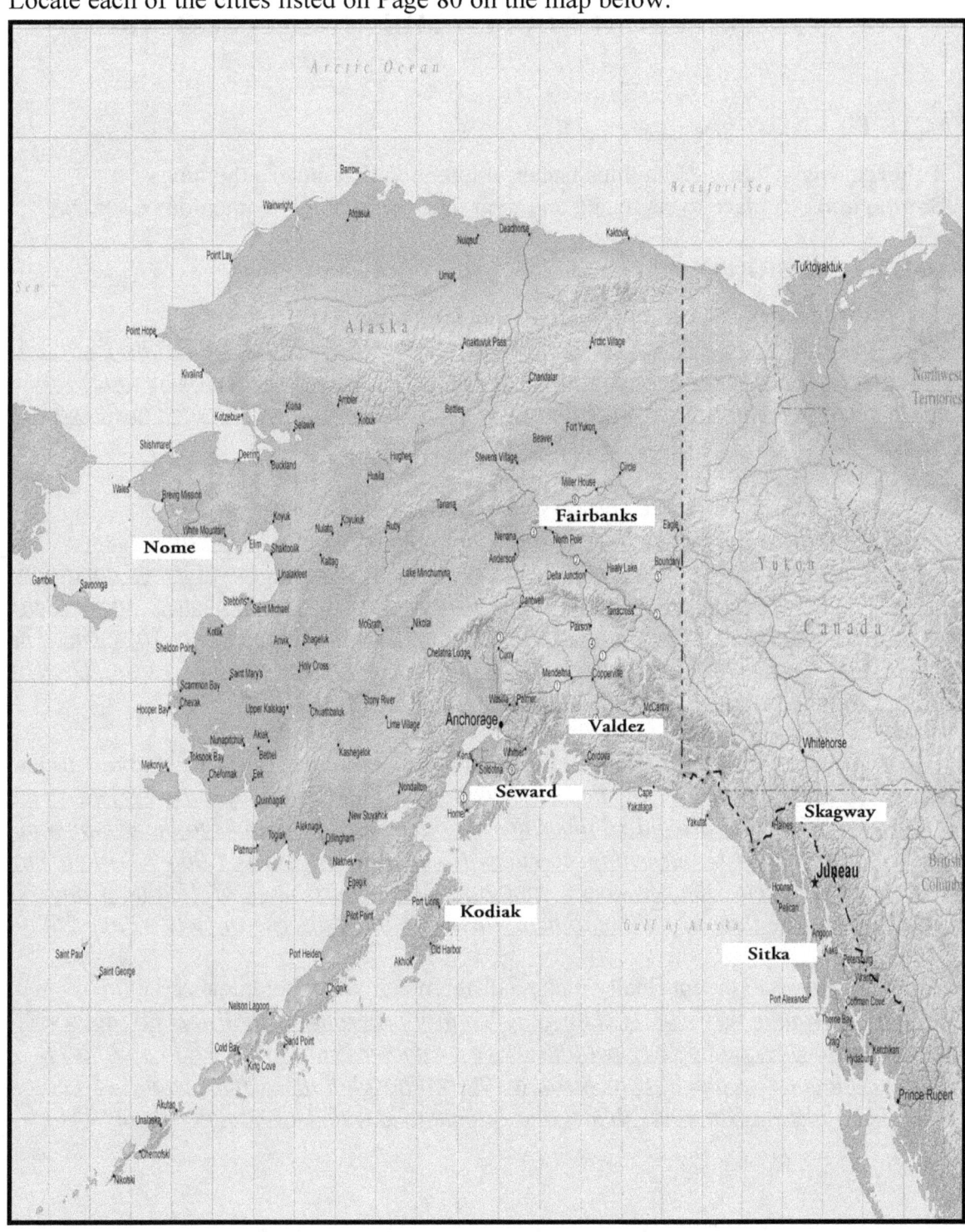

UNIT 6: COLD WAR ERA

LESSON 23: TUBERCULOSIS: THE ALASKA SCOURGE

FACTS TO KNOW

Tuberculosis –Highly contagious bacterial infection that attacks the lungs
Sanitarium – A place to segregate and treat those with highly contagious diseases

COMPREHENSION QUESTIONS

1) Why was tuberculosis especially dangerous for Native Alaskans?
Medical care was sparse and the conditions under which Native Alaskans lived was conducive to its spread. Segregation of active TB cases was not easy among Alaska Natives because families were large and lived together in small spaces – often sleeping in the same bed. (Pages 254-255)

2) When was Alaska's first sanatorium opened? What was it like?
Alaska's first sanatorium opened about three miles out of Skagway right after the war. The hospital was actually an abandoned U.S. Army complex, and nurses described conditions for the 90 patients as drafty. "Snow filtered through the plywood walls," nurse Betty Sorrels later recalled in a biographical sketch for the Juneau-Douglas City Museum. "The medical staff used canvas as bedspreads to aid in keeping the patients warm. The few windows were covered with a constant sheet of frost and ice." (Page 257)

3) How did Gov. Ernest Gruening help fight the tuberculosis crisis in Native Alaskan villages? *Alaska Territorial Gov. Ernest Gruening told legislators that the TB death rate for Alaska Natives was around 16 times the national average. Thanks to the eye-opening information provided by Gruening, territorial Sen. Edward Lewis "Bob" Bartlett and Dr. C. Earl Albrecht, the territory's first official Commissioner of Health, Congress appropriated more than $1 million to help Alaska fight the disease in 1949. (Page 260)*

4) How did the government finally make a difference in the tuberculosis crisis?
The Alaska Grant money was used to set up control programs, establish a TB register, administer vaccines and deliver health services. Another grant was used to build a TB facility at Mount Edgecumbe near Sitka, a 400-bed hospital in Anchorage and 25-bed hospitals at Barrow, Kotzebue, Bethel and Kanakanak, near Dillingham. (Pages 261-262)

DISCUSSION QUESTION

(Discuss this question with your teacher or write your answer in essay form below. Use additional paper if necessary.)

How was health care different for white Alaskans and Native Alaskans in the 1950s?

_____
_____
_____
_____
_____
_____
_____
_____
_____
_____
_____
_____
_____
_____
_____
_____

TIME TO REVIEW

Review Chapters 20-23 of your book before moving on the Unit Review. See how many questions you can answer without looking at your book.

Cold War Era
Crossword Puzzle

Read Across and Down clues and fill in blank boxes that match numbers on the clues

Across

1. Name of project that solved power problems in Anchorage area in 1950s
4. Electric cooperative that formed in 1950s in the Anchorage area
10. This disease, called the Alaska Scourge, ravaged Alaska Native villages during the 1940-50s
11. Resort built near Girdwood in 1954
15. An airline pilot compared Anchorage to this international city
20. Military dollars spent to improve this road that connected Valdez to Fairbanks helped Valdez' fishing community
21. Anchorage residents fooled a U.S. official in order to get this new government building built in 1930s
22. This is what Alaska children nicknamed floating clinics like the *M/V Hygiene*
24. Fairbanks dairy that had to close its doors when cheaper products and more variety began arriving in Alaska via the Alaska-Canada Highway
21. Anchorage's first television station that began broadcasting in 1953
28. By 1952, this was the fastest-growing city in North America
31. This highway that connects Resurrection Bay to Anchorage was completed in 1951
33. A vast, flat, treeless region in which the subsoil is permanently frozen
34. The nuns of this order built a new 52-bed hospital at Ninth Avenue and L Street in Anchorage in 1939

Down

1. Russian Jack remembered hunting this animal in what became downtown Anchorage
2. The U.S. military built a naval base on this island near Sitka
3. Code name for Alaska Integrated Communications Enterprise
5. People thought this Russian leader wanted to take over the world
6. Daily passenger service between Anchorage and Fairbanks began on June 18, 1951
8. The device that the USSR developed that frightened the world in late-1940s
9. Only six of 30 first-graders that contracted TB lived to finish out the 1941 school year in this northern village
11. Man behind Anchorage's first television station that began broadcasting in 1953
12. Air Force station near Nenana
13. The addition of a canal to connect Lake Hood and Lake Spenard made this waterway the world's largest base for these types of aircraft
14. Fear that gripped the nation following World War II when USSR became a rival was known as this
16. Wrecked ocean-going tanker that was used to provide about half the electricity needed for Anchorage during 1930s
11. One Southwest Alaska base that was reactivated in the 1950s to intercept Russian aircraft foraying into U.S. airspace

Cold War Era
Crossword Puzzle Key

18 Russian satellite launched in 1951
19 Anchorage radio station that went on the air in 1948
23 Alaska's first TB sanatorium was built near this Southeast town
25 New U.S. Air Force base built near Fairbanks during Cold War era
26 Fairbanks Air Force base
29 Anchorage Air Force base
30 Early warning system used this type of detection
32 This community became home to a chief U.S. Navy base during 1950s and quadrupled its population

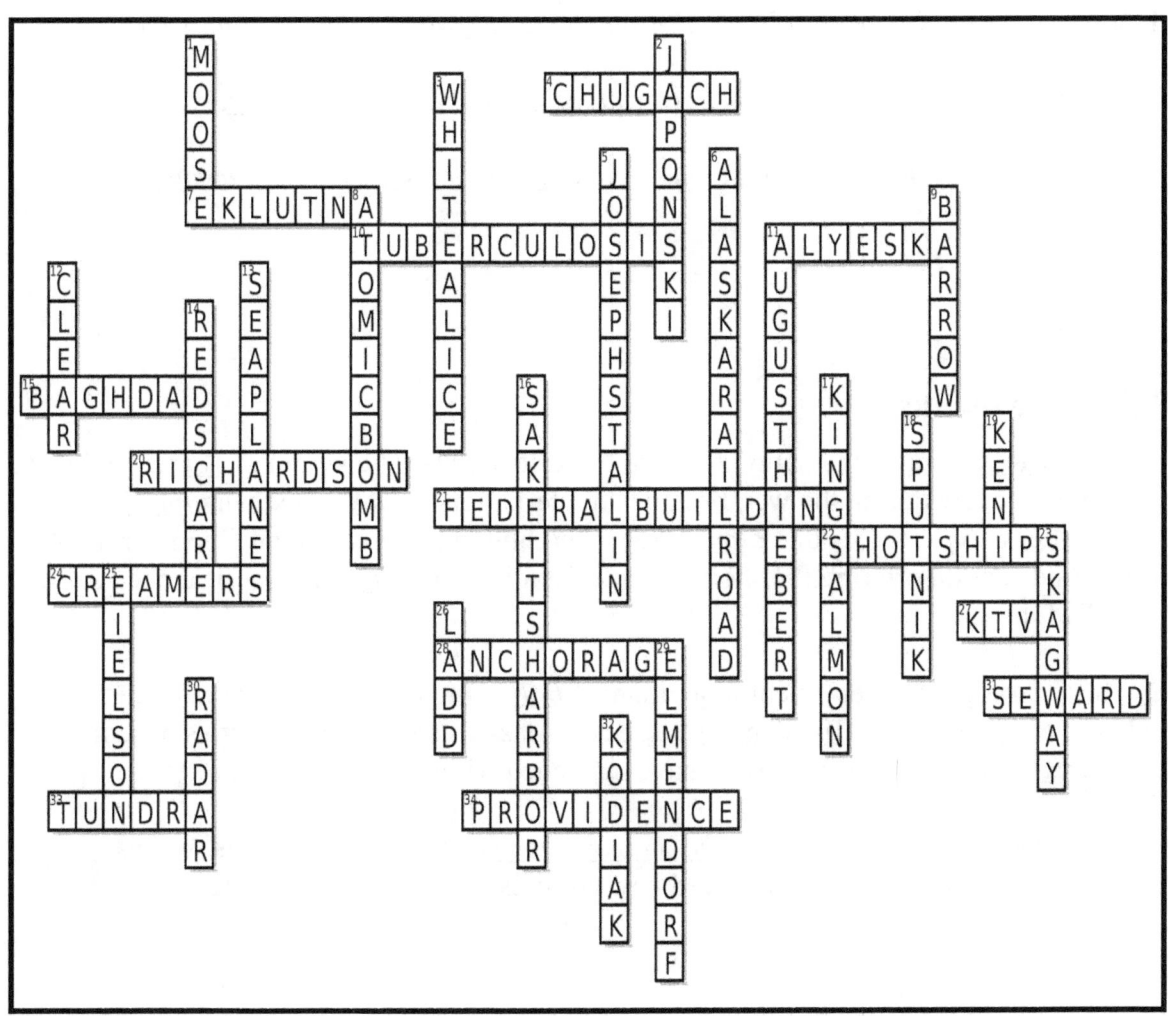

UNIT 6: COLD WAR ERA

REVIEW LESSONS 20-23

Write down what you remember about:

Union of Soviet Socialist Republics – *Rival of the United States with nuclear power*

Distant Early Warning System – *Radar network designed to warn Alaska of nuclear attack*

Anchorage Light and Power Co. – *Anchorage power company that had to increase production for the fast-increasing population*

Tundra – *A vast, flat, treeless region in which the subsoil is permanently frozen*

Tuberculosis – *Highly contagious bacterial infection that attacks the lungs*

Sanitarium – *A place to segregate and treat those with highly contagious diseases*

Fill in the blanks:

1) "*Red Scare*" gripped the nation following World War II. The Union of *Soviet Socialist Republics*, an ally during the war, became an international rival armed with *nuclear power* after it exploded its first *atomic bomb* and built an intercontinental bomber in late 1949. And Alaska, offering the shortest route for a Soviet *attack* on America, became the "*eyes*" of the nation.

2) The federal government spent more than *$1 billion* on an ultra-modern radar network, called the *Distant Early Warning System*. Soon Alaska's sparse communities became *connected* in a way that never could have happened without *military* money.

3) They also brought *television, radio and telephone* communications – as well as *interracial* marriages – that introduced new cultures to Native communities.

4) By the early 1950s, the tent city at the mouth of *Ship Creek* had turned into a bustling, modern city thanks to *federal money pouring in for military defense*.

5) The town which in 1947 didn't have one *traffic* light, found itself playing catch-up to a demand for *services and goods as frame houses popped up all over*. Reliable *power* for the growing populace soon became a major problem. *Blackouts* became frequent, prices were high and many homes had no *electricity* at all.

6) "An airline pilot, arriving over *Anchorage* at night after the long flight from Tokyo and seeing for the first time its pattern of flickering lights, winking like *jewels* in the midst of a vast, forbidding *wilderness*, described the city as a *"Tundra Baghdad."* In many respects, the name fits.

7) The National Municipal League and Look magazine named *Anchorage* an "*All-American City*" in 1956 for "successfully tackling a skyrocketing *population* that threatened to swamp city facilities and pushing for needed civic improvements." It was the first time that any city outside of the *contiguous 48 states* had been so honored.

8) *Tuberculosis* persisted in the remote villages partly because *medical care* was sparse and partly because the conditions under which *Alaska Natives* lived was conducive to its spread. Segregation of active *TB* cases was not easy among *Alaska Natives* because families were large and lived together in small spaces – often sleeping in the same bed.

9) Alaska *grant money* was used to set up control programs, establish a *TB register*, administer *vaccines* and deliver health services. Another *grant* was used to build a *TB facility* at Mount Edgecumbe near Sitka, a 400-bed hospital in Anchorage and 25-bed hospitals at *Barrow, Kotzebue, Bethel and Kanakanak, near Dillingham*.

UNIT 6: COLD WAR ERA

UNIT TEST

Choose *two* of the following questions to answer in paragraph form. Use as much detail as possible to completely answer the question.

1) How did the "red scare" put a spotlight on Alaska? How did it change Alaska?

2) Why did Anchorage's population increase dramatically in the 1950s? What problems did the city face because of the influx of people to the city?

3) Name two other Alaska towns that grew during the 1950s. How did these towns benefit by the defense spending during the 1950s?

4) Describe the tuberculosis crisis for Alaska Natives. Why was it so much worse for Alaska Natives than non-Natives? How did the government get involved in stopping the epidemic?

TEACHER NOTES ABOUT THIS UNIT

UNIT 7: ROAD TO STATEHOOD

LESSON 24: MOVERS & SHAKERS

FACTS TO KNOW

    Judge James Wickersham – Introduced the first statehood bill for Alaska in 1916
    Organic Act of 1884 – Allowed Alaska to become a civil and judicial territory
    John Kinkead – Alaska's first governor, appointed by U.S. President Chester Arthur in 1884

COMPREHENSION QUESTIONS

1) What was the result of Alaska's first statehood bill in 1916? Why?
Alaska only had about 58,000 residents when Wickersham introduced the first statehood bill in 1916. The bill didn't go anywhere, however, because most members of Congress, as well as the American public, thought Alaska wasn't ready for admittance to the Union. (Page 265)

2) What event caused the government to pay more attention to Alaska in 1880?
In 1880 prospectors discovered rich veins of gold on Douglas Island, across from what became Juneau in Southeast Alaska. Hundreds of white miners headed north. Those newcomers clamored for Congress to set up a civilian government so they could stake mining claims and get title to land. (Page 256)

3) What did the Organic Act of 1884 provide Alaska?
Through the Organic Act of 1884, Congress provided Alaska with the bare essentials of government. It did not authorize a legislature, but it did make Sitka the temporary capital and allowed for a district court, a governor, a district attorney and a U.S. marshal. (Page 266)

4) According to political scientist Melvin Crain, what were the responsibilities of the first governors of Alaska?
According to political scientist Melvin Crain, they had little to do. The first governors "had practically no civil duties to perform except to inspect, report and to enforce a handful of contradictory laws, with no enforcement means provided," according to Crain. (Page 267)

5) Describe the Civil Code of 1900 that Congress adopted after the Klondike gold rush.
Following the Klondike Gold Rush near the turn-of-the-last century, Congress adopted a new civil code that allowed communities of 300 or more to incorporate with seven-member city councils and three-member school boards. The Civil Code of 1900 also set up new judicial districts, specified what activities were illegal and assigned punishments for violations. (Page 267)

6) What were some of Judge Wickersham's accomplishments that benefited Alaska?
Among Wickersham's accomplishments are winning home rule for Alaska as a territory in 1912, obtaining funds for construction of the Alaska Railroad in 1914, opening the Alaska Agricultural College and School of Mining in 1917 – which later became the University of Alaska – and introducing the first statehood bill in 1916, 43 years before it became a reality. (Pages 268-269)

DISCUSSION QUESTION

(Discuss this question with your teacher or write your answer in essay form below. Use additional paper if necessary.)

Why was statehood important to Alaskans?

_____
_____
_____
_____
_____
_____
_____
_____
_____
_____
_____
_____
_____

ENRICHMENT ACTIVITY

Look for the book *Frontier Politics: Alaska's James Wickersham* by Evangeline Atwood at your local library. After you have read it, write a one-page report about what you learned.

LEARN MORE

Frontier Politics: Alaska's James Wickersham. Evangeline Atwood. Portland, Oregon: Binford & Mort, 1979.

UNIT 7: ROAD TO STATEHOOD

LESSON 25: STATEHOOD MOMENTUM BUILDS

FACTS TO KNOW

Territorial Gov. Ernest Gruening – Alaska's territorial governor from 1939-1953
Edward Lewis "Bob" Bartlett – Elected the territory's official delegate to Congress

COMPREHENSION QUESTIONS

1) Why did some oppose statehood for Alaska?
Those in opposition included powerful outside fishing, shipping and mining companies that held monopolies in the territory and flowed profits to the Lower 48. There also were some influential Alaskans who didn't want to change the status quo – including one of the territory's first industrialists, Austin Lathrop. (Page 273)

2) Why was Austin "Cap" Lathrop opposed to statehood? Why did his successor, C.W. Snedden, endorse statehood?
Lathrop believed that statehood would bring more expenses than the residents could bear. Lathrop, who owned mines, radio stations, theaters and other businesses in the Last Frontier, didn't want to pay more taxes, which would decrease his profits. Snedden, the new publisher, endorsed statehood and printed a special supplement dedicated to its merits. "Give Americans the full privileges of American citizenship," Snedden wrote. "Turn Alaska's destiny over to Alaskans." (Page 274)

3) What events changed Gov. Ernest Gruening's opinion about statehood?
First, Edward Lewis "Bob" Bartlett, running on a statehood platform in 1944, won the right to represent Alaska as the new non-voting delegate to Congress. Then President Harry S. Truman, in his 1946 State of the Union address, said that statehood should be granted once the federal government knew how Alaskans stood on the issue. When voters in the territory passed a statewide referendum on statehood by a vote of 9,630 to 6,822 in a special election held later that year, Gruening became a champion for the cause. (Pages 275-276)

4) What did Gov. Gruening do to try to get statehood for Alaska?
He organized a "committee of 100" prominent Americans who supported Alaska's aspirations. Supporters included U.S. President Franklin D. Roosevelt's wife, Eleanor, actor James Cagney and author Pearl S. Buck. (Pages 276)

5) Did President Harry S. Truman support statehood for Alaska? What did he tell Congress about the issue?
Yes. "Alaska is our last great frontier area and has the capacity to provide new opportunities for many thousands of our citizens. It contains known resources of food, timber, and minerals of great value to the national economy, and may have much greater resources as yet undiscovered. ... "I believe, therefore, that we should admit Alaska to statehood at the earliest possible date, and I urge the Congress to enact the necessary legislation. ..." (Pages 276-277)

6) How did the statehood bill get shut down by the Senate?
A statehood bill did pass the House by a vote of 186-146 but was killed in the Senate by a coalition of conservative Republicans and Southern Democrats – the Republicans feared Alaskans would elect two Democrats to the Senate, tipping the scales of power, and the Southern Democrats feared Alaskan senators would tip the balance on civil rights issues. (Page 279)

DISCUSSION QUESTION

(Discuss this question with your teacher or write your answer in essay form below. Use additional paper if necessary.)

Many Alaskans fought hard to convince the government to grant statehood. Can you think of another time in history when people banded together to make an important change in the world?

_____
_____
_____
_____
_____
_____
_____

ENRICHMENT ACTIVITY

Imagine that you are a resident of Alaska living in the early 1900s. Write a persuasive letter to the U.S. president about why Alaska should have statehood. Include at least three detailed points to support your stance.

LEARN MORE

Alaska's Quest for Statehood 1867-1959. Robert A. Frederick. Anchorage: Anchorage Silver Anniversary Task Force, Municipality of Anchorage, 1985.

UNIT 7: ROAD TO STATEHOOD

LESSON 26: EGAN: THE FINAL PUSH

FACTS TO KNOW

William Allen Egan – Chairman of the Constitutional Convention and Alaska's first elected state governor; he was born in Valdez

Anthony J. Dimond – Alaska's non-voting delegate to Congress from 1932-1944

Constitutional Convention – Meeting of 55 volunteers from all walks of life in Fairbanks in 1955-1956 to draft a constitution for what they hoped would be a new state of Alaska

Frank Peratrovich – A Tlingit Indian from Southeast Alaska, and the only member of the Constitutional Convention that was Alaska Native, he was elected vice chairman of the Convention held in Fairbanks in 1955-1956

Alaska-Tennessee Plan – Provided Alaska with two senators and one representative to Congress; the same plan was used by Tennessee in 1796 to gain admission to the Union

COMPREHENSION QUESTIONS

1) How did William Egan get involved in politics?
He learned about American politics by faithfully reading the Congressional Record during Dimond's stint in Washington, D.C. He also followed weekly Valdez Miner columns submitted by Dimond's secretary, Edward Lewis "Bob" Bartlett. Following in his godfather's Democratic Party footsteps, Egan won a seat in the Territorial House of Representatives in 1940. (Page 281)

2) Summarize Anthony Dimond's vision of Alaska as a state?
He stated that the following steps were necessary to secure a place as the 49th star: (1) presentation by the Territorial Legislature of a petition to Congress voicing the people's request for statehood; (2) passage of an Enabling Act by Congress authorizing the people of Alaska, through a constitutional convention, to draw up a state constitution; (3) submission of this constitution to the people of the Territory, and upon its approval; (4) submission to Congress, whereupon by a resolution of that body, the Territory can be declared to be a State. (Pages 281-282)

3) What qualifications did William Egan have to be elected president of the Constitutional Convention?
His diplomatic skills, as well as knowledge of parliamentary procedures, proved to be invaluable as the group hammered out the details of what became a 14,400-word document. (Page 283)

4) What were some of the terms of the state constitution that the delegates signed in 1956?
It provided for a strong governor, appointed judiciary and a legislature that included 20 senators elected to four-year terms and 40 representatives to serve two-year terms. It also delayed action on Native land claims, gave the vote to 19-year-olds and declared that resources were to be managed and developed for the benefit of all people. (Page 284)

5) Explain how the Alaska-Tennessee plan got its name? What was unique about the way that Alaska's prospective congressmen traveled to Washington D.C.?
The Alaska-Tennessee Plan, which provided for representation in Washington, D.C., got its name because it was used by Tennessee in 1796 to gain admission to the Union and provided for the election of two senators and one representative to send to Congress. Tennessee sent them via horseback to the nation's capital. Alaska's representatives traveled by car. (Pages 286-287)

DISCUSSION QUESTION

(Discuss this question with your teacher or write your answer in essay form below. Use additional paper if necessary.)

How do you think Alaska would be different today if it never achieved statehood?

_____
_____
_____
_____
_____
_____
_____
_____
_____
_____
_____
_____
_____
_____
_____
_____
_____
_____

TIME TO REVIEW

Review Chapters 24-26 of your book before moving on the Unit Review. See how many questions you can answer without looking at your book.

UNIT 7: ROAD TO STATEHOOD

REVIEW LESSONS 24-26

Write down what you remember about:

Judge James Wickersham – *Introduced the first statehood bill for Alaska in 1916*

Organic Act of 1884 – *Allowed Alaska to become a civil and judicial territory*

John Kinkead – *Alaska's first governor, appointed by U.S. President Chester Arthur in 1884*

Territorial Gov. Ernest Gruening – *Alaska's territorial governor from 1939-1953*

Edward Lewis "Bob" Bartlett – *Elected the territory's official delegate to Congress*

William Allen Egan – *Chairman of the Constitutional Convention and Alaska's first elected state governor; he was born in Valdez*

Anthony J. Dimond – *Alaska's non-voting delegate to Congress from 1932-1944*

Constitutional Convention – *Meeting of 55 volunteers from all walks of life in Fairbanks in 1955-1956 to draft a constitution for what they hoped would be a new state of Alaska*

Frank Peratrovich – *A Tlingit Indian from Southeast Alaska, and the only member of the Constitutional Convention that was Alaska Native, he was elected vice chairman of the Convention held in Fairbanks in 1955-1956*

Alaska-Tennessee Plan – *Provided Alaska with two senators and one representative to Congress; the same plan was used by Tennessee in 1796 to gain admission to the Union*

Fill in the blanks:

1) Through the *Organic Act of 1884*, Congress provided Alaska with the bare essentials of government. It did not authorize a legislature, but it did make *Sitka* the temporary capital and allowed for a *district court, a governor, a district attorney and a U.S. marshal.*

2) Among Judge *James Wickersham's* accomplishments are winning home rule for Alaska as a *territory* in 1912, obtaining funds for construction of the *Alaska Railroad* in 1914, opening the *Alaska Agricultural College and School of Mining* in 1917 – which later became the *University of Alaska* – and introducing the first *statehood* bill in 1916, 43 years before it became a reality.

3) Proponents reasoned that statehood would allow Alaska to raise *tax revenues* and take over management of its *fisheries*. It also could establish a state-managed *police* force and state-appointed *judiciary*. In addition, Alaskans would get two *voting* members in the U.S. Senate and one in the House of Representatives.

4) Those in opposition included powerful outside *fishing, shipping and mining* companies that held monopolies in the territory and flowed profits to the *Lower 48*. There also were some influential Alaskans who didn't want to change the status quo – including *Austin "Cap" Lathrop*, who owned the Fairbanks Daily News Miner.

5) *Ernest Gruening*, an Easterner appointed as Alaska's *territorial governor* from 1939-1953, became convinced that the only way Alaska would get adequate *roads, airfields and hospitals*, and settle *aboriginal* rights, was to have elected, *voting* representatives in Congress.

6) *William Egan*, the godson of Anthony J. Dimond, learned about American politics by faithfully reading the *Congressional Record* during Dimond's stint in Washington, D.C. He also followed weekly Valdez Miner columns submitted by Dimond's secretary, *Edward Lewis "Bob" Bartlett*, who became Alaska's delegate in 1944. Following in his godfather's Democratic Party footsteps, *Egan* won a seat in the Territorial House of Representatives in 1940.

7) *William Egan* drafted the legislation calling for a 75-day *convention* to be held on the campus of the University of Alaska in College, near Fairbanks, in November *1955*. He led the group in drafting Alaska's first *state constitution*.

8) Sen-elect *William Egan* and Rep-elect Rivers traveled to Washington D.C. as part of the *Alaska-Tennessee* plan, which was used by *Tennessee* in 1796 to gain admission to the Union. It provided for the election of two *senators* and one *representative* to send to Congress.

Courtesy Alaska State Library

From left, Senator-elect Ernest Gruening, Martha Rivers, Representative-elect Ralph Rivers, Neva Egan and Senator-elect William Egan stand by the car that the Rivers and Egans drove all the way to the East Coast in order to present Congress with Alaska's newly drafted 15-article constitution and Alaska-Tennessee Plan. They left Fairbanks on Dec. 10, 1956, and arrived in Washington, D.C., three weeks later. The group averaged 300 miles a day with only snow tires, no chains, in 60-below-zero temperatures.

Road to Statehood
Word Search Puzzle Key
Find the words listed below

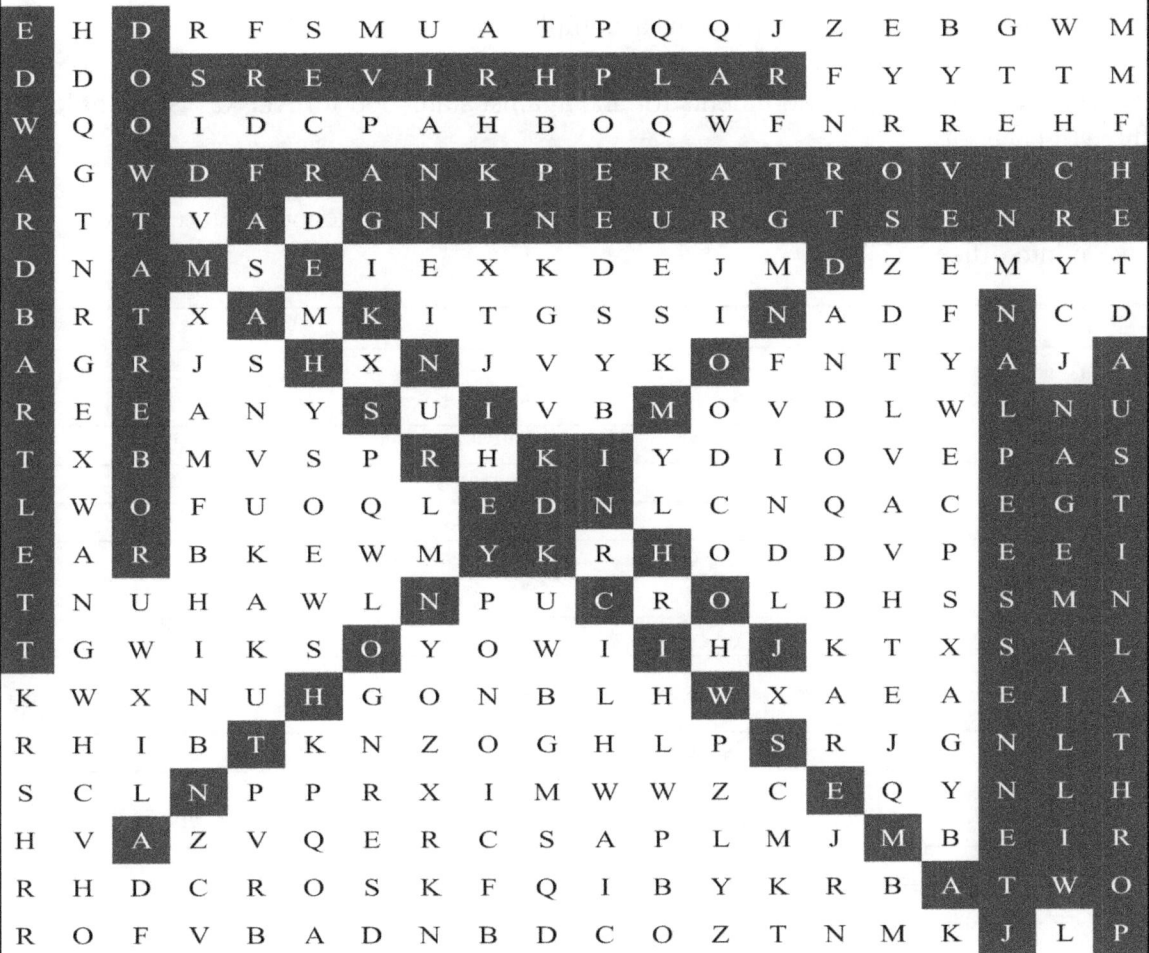

WILLIAM EGAN JAMES WICKERSHAM ANTHONY DIMOND
JOHN KINKEAD EDWARD BARTLETT AUSTIN LATHROP
ERNEST GRUENING ROBERT ATWOOD FRANK PERATROVICH
RALPH RIVERS TENNESSEE PLAN

UNIT 7: ROAD TO STATEHOOD

UNIT TEST

Choose *two* of the following questions to answer in paragraph form. Use as much detail as possible to completely answer the question.

1) Why was Judge James Wickersham considered one of the most influential Alaskans in history? Write about at least two of his accomplishments.

2) What were some of the arguments for and against statehood for Alaska? Share at least three of each.

3) How did William Egan make a difference in the fight for statehood before he was sworn into office?

TEACHER NOTES ABOUT THIS UNIT

UNIT 8: STATEHOOD AT LAST

LESSON 27: BLACK GOLD TIPS THE BALANCE

FACTS TO KNOW

Kenai Peninsula – Where the discovery of oil began the petroleum boom
Thomas White – Known as the "Sourdough Driller" because he drilled the first producing oil well in Alaska
Katalla – City in the Kenai Peninsula that boomed after the first oil fields were discovered

COMPREHENSION QUESTIONS

1) Name two groups of people that discovered oil in Alaska before 1957. What did these groups use it for?
Alaska Natives used the black wealth oozing out of the hills and beaches long before white men found their way north. Eskimos burned the tar-like chips, Southeastern Natives used it for war paint and others used oil shale to make knives and labrets. The Russians also knew of Alaska Peninsula oil seeps as early as 1860, but since whale oil was the important fuel at the time, oil from rocks was ignored. (Page 290)

2) How did Thomas White find the first producing oil field in Alaska?
In 1896, trapper Thomas White was bear hunting in the Controller Bay region near Katalla, about 47 miles southeast of Cordova. While tracking a wounded animal, he fell into thick, black mud seeping up from the ground. After cleaning his gun and himself, he tossed a match into the pit "to see what would happen," he later said. The pool burst into flames and burned for a month. (Page 291)

3) How did the 1920 Mineral Leasing Act change the oil rush in Alaska?
The 1920 Mineral Leasing Act ushered in another oil rush. During the first six months of enactment, 178 applications covering 386,673 acres were filed in the Juneau land office. When Alaska had been re-opened to oil seekers, only 40 wells had been drilled in the whole territory, all but nine in the Katalla area. But now there was a renewal of interest in the Alaska Peninsula area. (Page 294)

4) What did Cook Inlet oil provide for Alaskans?
Cook Inlet oil provided Alaskans with gasoline, diesel fuel, heating oil and jet fuel. And a pipeline, built beneath Turnagain Arm, carried natural gas from the Kenai Peninsula to heat Anchorage homes and businesses. (Page 295)

DISCUSSION QUESTION

(Discuss this question with your teacher or write your answer in essay form below. Use additional paper if necessary.)

What would your everyday life be like without oil?

ENRICHMENT ACTIVITY

Watch this short YouTube video about oil discoveries in Alaska: https://www.youtube.com/watch?v=LJgXgHh6las

LEARN MORE

Read more about the discovery of oil in Alaska by visiting http://www.akhistorycourse.org/modern-alaska/oil-discovery-and-development-in-alaska

UNIT 8: STATEHOOD AT LAST

LESSON 28: WE'RE IN!

FACTS TO KNOW

Theodore F. "Ted" Stevens – Young attorney who served as a coordinator for Alaska and Hawaii statehood movements

U.S. President Dwight Eisenhower – Signed the official papers to make Alaska the 49th state in 1959

COMPREHENSION QUESTIONS

1) When did Alaska officially become a state?
<u>Although Congress approved statehood for Alaska on June 30, 1958, it took six months for Alaskan's to hold elections for leaders. Alaska officially became a state on Jan. 3, 1959. (Pages 296, 302)</u>

2) How did the appointment of Fred Seaton as Secretary of the Interior in 1956 help the cause of statehood?
<u>The appointment of sympathetic Nebraska newspaper publisher Fred Seaton as Secretary of the Interior in 1956 helped sway the opinion of the Eisenhower administration toward statehood. Previously, Eisenhower had endorsed splitting Alaska into two states. (Page 300)</u>

3) What did Theodore Stevens do to help Alaska receive statehood?
<u>Stevens, who became known as "Mr. Alaska" for decades of service as a U.S. senator, served as coordinator of the Alaska and Hawaii statehood movements with the now pro-statehood Secretary of Interior and helped draft the statehood act. He was instrumental in getting language in the act that persuaded President Dwight D. Eisenhower to support the bill. (Page 301)</u>

4) Name two other things that helped Alaska achieve statehood?
<u>By 1957, Southern senators who had previously opposed admitting both Alaska and Hawaii as states because they feared new senators would not be sympathetic to segregation, knew the tide had turned. Anti-segregation forces already had a clear majority. And the discovery of a large oil field in the Kenai Peninsula that December proved that Alaska probably would be able to carry its own economic weight. (Page 301)</u>

5) What were some of the tasks that William Egan had to handle after being elected as Alaska's first governor?
He and lieutenant governor, Hugh Wade, had to create a court system, public works department, fish and game management – one of the state's first acts was to abolish the much-hated use of fish traps – and figure out how to take control of the state's abundant natural resources. (Pages 304-305)

6) What happened to him shortly after he took the oath of office?
Egan, who had become ill a month earlier, immediately left for surgery following his swearing in ceremony on Jan. 3. He checked into St. Ann's Hospital in Juneau and underwent surgery to remove his gall bladder and a gallstone. Instead of recovering, however, his condition worsened. While Egan did rally, his healing was slow. So the burden of governing fell on Wade's shoulders for the first few months of statehood. (Pages 307-308)

DISCUSSION QUESTION

(Discuss this question with your teacher or write your answer in essay form below. Use additional paper if necessary.)

Why did many people pity William Egan when he was elected as Alaska's first governor?

ENRICHMENT ACTIVITY

Using what you've learned from Units 6 and 7, create a timeline of events that led to Alaska gaining statehood in 1959.

LEARN MORE

A History of Alaska Statehood. Claus-M. Naske. Maryland: University Press of America, 1985.

UNIT 8: STATEHOOD AT LAST

LESSON 29: 'SIMPLE FLAG OF THE LAST FRONTIER'

FACTS TO KNOW

John Ben "Benny" Benson – Designed Alaska's flag in 1920
Willow ptarmigan – Official state bird of Alaska
Forget-me-not – Official state flower of Alaska
Alaska's Flag – Official song of Alaska written by Marie Drake

COMPREHENSION QUESTIONS

1) Where did Benny Benson grow up? What was he like as a young boy?
Benson, born in Chignik in 1913, lost his mother when he was 4. His father, a Swedish fox farmer, did not know how to take care of little boys. He put Benny and his brother, Carl, into the Jesse Lee Mission Home, established by Methodist missionaries in 1890 and named for a Methodist preacher. Benny was a thoughtful youngster, with strangely mature insight even before he was old enough to go to school. (Pages 312-313)

2) When did Benny Benson become fascinated with the stars?
Benny felt homesick when he moved to the mainland in 1926, but he soon found that Seward had one great advantage over Unalaska, where thick fog had often obscured the stars overhead. The youngster went wild with delight and often stayed outdoors in the evenings, star-gazing, dreaming dreams and thinking deep thoughts. (Page 314)

3) How old was he when he designed the flag? Explain how his design was chosen.
Benny was 13 years old when his seventh-grade teacher announced the territory-wide contest for school children to design a flag for Alaska. His design of eight stars on a field of blue was the unanimous winner. (Pages 314-315)

4) How did he explain his design on his entry?
"The blue field is for Alaska's skies and the forget-me-not, an Alaskan flower. The North Star is for the future state of Alaska, the most northerly of the Union. The Dipper is for the Great Bear, symbolizing strength," Benson scribbled. (Page 315)

5) How was Benny Benson honored for his design, and then later at the signing of Alaska's constitution?
He won prize money and a watch for his design. At the signing of Alaska's Constitution in 1956, he was introduced to the audience as the designer of Alaska's flag. (Pages 316-317)

DISCUSSION QUESTION

(Discuss this question with your teacher or write your answer in essay form below. Use additional paper if necessary.)

If you were asked to design the flag of Alaska, how would you draw it?

_____
_____
_____
_____
_____
_____
_____
_____
_____
_____
_____
_____
_____
_____
_____
_____
_____
_____

TIME TO REVIEW

Review Chapters 27-29 of your book before moving on the Unit Review. See how many questions you can answer without looking at your book.

Statehood At Last
Word Scramble Puzzle Key
Unscramble the words below

1.	atdhtsoeo	statehood	What Alaska officially achieved on Jan. 3, 1959
2.	hwitgd seinoreewh	dwight eisenhower	U.S. President who signed the Alaska Statehood Bill
3.	etd sensetv	ted stevens	Young attorney who became known as "Mr. Alaska"
4.	lmailiw aeng	william egan	Alaska's first elected governor
5.	daewdr eatrtltb	edward bartlett	One of two first elected Alaska senators
6.	rtsene rgnuneig	ernest gruening	One of two first elected Alaska senators
7.	rpahl sevrri	ralph rivers	First elected Alaska congressman
8.	huhg aewd	hugh wade	First Alaska lieutenant governor
9.	otebrr owdoat	robert atwood	Editor of the Anchorage Daily Times
10.	eatiiooarzgnnr llbi	reorganization bill	This bill allowed the governor to appoint 12 commissioners for state departments

Statehood At Last
Word Scramble Puzzle Key
Unscramble the words below

#	Scrambled	Answer	Clue
1.	vrroognes osnmani	governors mansion	Place where the Egan family lived in Juneau following statehood
2.	gaiiirnv nosma	virginia mason	Hospital in Seattle where Gov. Egan underwent surgery after taking office
3.	yebnn onnesb	benny benson	Designer of the Alaska flag
4.	reiam eakdr	marie drake	Author of the Alaska Flag song
5.	irnoel deusurbny	elinor dusenbury	Creator of the melody for the Alaska Flag song
6.	olloap	apollo	Alaska's flag flew to the moon on board the 11th version of this spacecraft in July 1969 (when the first two humans actually walked on the moon)
7.	egoerg pkasr	george parks	Alaska territorial governor who initiated the flag contest for Alaska's school children
8.	ssjee ele	jesse lee	Home where Alaska's flag designer grew up
9.	fldoy niteugr	floyd guertin	Alaska's first commissioner of administration
10.	dvzael	valdez	Town where Alaska's first elected governor was born

UNIT 8: STATEHOOD AT LAST

REVIEW LESSONS 27-29

Write down what you remember about:

Kenai Peninsula – *Where the discovery of oil began the petroleum boom*

Thomas White – *Known as the "Sourdough Driller" because he drilled the first producing oil well in Alaska*

Katalla – *City in the Kenai Peninsula that boomed after the first oil fields were discovered*

Theodore F. "Ted" Stevens – *Young attorney who served as a coordinator for Alaska and Hawaii statehood movements*

U.S. President Dwight Eisenhower – *Signed the official papers to make Alaska the 49th state in 1959*

John Ben "Benny" Benson – *Designed Alaska's flag in 1920*

Willow ptarmigan – *Official state bird of Alaska*

Forget-me-not – *Official state flower of Alaska*

Alaska's Flag – *Official song of Alaska written by Marie Drake*

Fill in the blanks:

1) In 1896, trapper *Thomas White* was bear hunting in the Controller Bay region near *Katalla*. He fell into thick, black mud seeping up from the ground. After cleaning his gun and himself, he *tossed a match into the pit* "to see what would happen," he later said. The pool *burst into flames and burned* for a month. It became the first producing *oil field* discovered in Alaska.

2) *Cook Inlet* oil provided Alaskans with *gasoline, diesel fuel, heating oil and jet fuel*. And a *pipeline*, built beneath Turnagain Arm, carried natural *gas* from the Kenai Peninsula to heat Anchorage homes and businesses.

3) By 1957, *southern* senators who had previously opposed admitting both Alaska and Hawaii as states because they feared new senators would not be sympathetic to *segregation*, knew the tide had turned. Anti-*segregation* forces already had a clear majority.

4) And the discovery of a large *oil field* in the *Kenai* Peninsula that December proved that Alaska probably would be able to carry its own *economic* weight.

5) U.S. President *Dwight D. Eisenhower* signed the official papers to make Alaska the *49th state* on Jan. 3, *1959*.

6) Alaskans love their *flag*, designed by half-Aleut *John Ben "Benny" Benson* in the 1920s. Its simple design of *eight stars on a field of blue* came from *Benson*'s love of the *star-studded skies* found in his homeland.

7) Perhaps his fascination with those distant twinkling stars inspired the *13*-year-old *Benny* when his *seventh-grade* teacher announced the territory-wide contest for school children to *design a flag* for Alaska.

UNIT 8: STATEHOOD AT LAST

UNIT TEST

Choose *two* of the following questions to answer in paragraph form. Use as much detail as possible to completely answer the question.

1) Who were the first groups of people to use oil in Alaska? What did they use it for? How did the "discovery" of oil in the Kenai Peninsula change Alaska?

2) Write a short summary of how Alaska officially became a state. What events led to the official signing of the documents by President Eisenhower in January 1959?

3) How was the design for Alaska's flag chosen? Who was the designer? How did he explain his design?

TEACHER NOTES ABOUT THIS UNIT

TEACHER NOTES

TEACHER NOTES

TEACHER NOTES

www.ingramcontent.com/pod-product-compliance
Lightning Source LLC
Chambersburg PA
CBHW082127230426
43671CB00015B/2826